At Bat #3

Munson ★ Garvey
Brock ★ Carew

by Bill Gutman

tempo
books

GROSSET & DUNLAP
Publishers • New York

For Elizabeth

Copyright © 1976 by Bill Gutman
All rights reserved
Library of Congress Catalogue Card Number: 75-39515
ISBN: 0-448-12270-7 (Tempo Edition)
ISBN: 0-448-13505-1 (Library Edition)

A Tempo Books Original
Tempo Books is registered in the U.S. Patent Office

Published simultaneously in Canada
Printed in the United States of America

CONTENTS

Thurman Munson

One day not so long ago, Thurman Munson sat down, thought a minute, then put his thoughts into words for a waiting reporter.

"Well, it's this way," he said. "I'm little. I'm pudgy. I don't look good doing things. Those big, tall guys look super."

To anyone who didn't know better, this would sound like the talk of a fringe player—a guy struggling to hang on, a player lacking in confidence who feels that he's about to lose his job or that he won't be given a fair shot at a position. It sounds like a player lacking the physical equipment to be a major league ballplayer.

But the words come from a superstar, a player considered one of the five best all-around catchers in the big leagues. In fact, there are those who rate him just a step or two behind the great Johnny Bench.

Little? At 5'-11", 190 pounds, Thurman Munson is not small.

Pudgy? Well, wasn't there a time when catchers were supposed to be built like rock-hard fireplugs? Heck, Yogi Berra didn't exactly remind people of John Wayne.

Doesn't look good doing things? In whose opinion? The fact is that he does everything well.

Those big, tall guys look super? Well, in this media image-conscious world, most of us want to be something we're not.

The point is this. Thurman Munson is an all-star; to many he is the best catcher in the American League. He plays for the New York Yankees, which is no longer the glamour team it once was but is still a magnetic, charismatic force for youngsters all over the country. He recently completed the best all-around season of a fine career, finishing 1975 with a .318 batting average and 102 runs batted in. He was the starting catcher in the All-Star Game and the number-one backstop on most American League all-league teams. Yet Thurman Munson feels neglected and unappreciated by the fans, and this bugs him.

There are several reasons for this neglect. One is Munson's basic nature. He's just not a flashy, outgoing guy. He plays hard—very hard—and is determined to win. So when he loses it takes him a while to get over it, and he often appears surly and sullen to members of the press. Thus he hasn't received the same amount of ink as the more outgoing players.

Another reason is Carlton Fisk. Fisk is the man Munson was referring to when he said "those big, tall guys look super." Fisk is the catcher for the American League-champion Boston Red Sox and Thurman's main rival for the league's top receiver. Fisk was American League Rookie of the Year in 1972, two years after Thurman had won the same distinction. But Fisk is tall, dark, handsome, and outgoing, and as a rookie he hit a brace of homers over Fenway Park's short left-field wall. So to most, he was immediately the young superstar catcher of the league. And Munson? Well, he just kind of become "Thurman Who?".

Munson's own annoyance started in 1973. Fisk was not having a good year. Munson was. Yet when the fans voted for the all-star catcher, Fisk won the position by some half million votes. Munson began brooding about his popularity and his image in the eyes of the fans.

But don't get Thurman Munson wrong. When he talks down about himself, he's talking strictly image, not ability. He has confidence in his ability, knows what he can do, and is proud of it. So do his teammates. They once decided to kid him and told him there was a rumor that Johnny Bench was being traded to the Yanks. Without blinking an eye, Thurman said:

"Bench coming to the Yankees? Hey, that's great for us. Where's he gonna play? Designated hitter?"

Munson knows he can compete with anyone behind the plate. In fact, had he played at another time, he might well have been *the* superstar at the position, and it wouldn't have mattered what kind of image he projected. Catcher used to be the position nobody wanted, but in the last decade or so, the position has been glamourized and has come into vogue. Many youngsters are now actually preparing by choice to become catchers.

There was a time when the game's great catchers could be counted on the fingertips. There were so few, and that covered maybe a half century of major league baseball. The real old timers will name the likes of Roger Bresnahan, Ray Schalk, and Gabby Street, yet they set no great records and left behind few remarkable achievements. When you mention the great players of those early days—Cobb, Wagner, Collins, Lajoie, Speaker, Jackson, Sisler, Ruth—none of them were catchers. The really good ones didn't want to go back there and take that pounding.

In the middle years of the game—the twenties, thirties, and forties—three names dominate: Gabby Hartnett, Bill Dickey, and Mickey Cochrane. These three Hall of Famers stood head and shoulders above the others and were considered the great catchers of their day and perhaps of all time. Each could handle himself behind the plate, and more importantly, each could hit. They were also great team leaders.

Then in the late forties and through the fifties, the catching position was once again basked in anonymity. Only two names really come up when anyone is talking about the catchers of that day, and they almost always go together. They are Berra and Campanella, Yogi of the Yankees, and Campy of the Dodgers. Like Dickey, Cochrane, and Hartnett, Yogi and Campy could do it all—catch, handle pitchers, hit, hit with power, lead. Both, too, are now enshrined in the Cooperstown Hall of Fame.

But think about Berra and Campanella for a minute. Both of them were also prototype of what a catcher should have been in those days. Both were short and stocky, powerfully built, but not exactly movie-star types. They seemed perfectly suited to squatting behind home plate and taking the pounding that goes with playing there. For a long time, most catchers seemed to resemble to some extent Berra and Campanella.

When coaches looked around they'd often pick the slowest, fattest kid to play catcher, because he could do little else and could use his bulk to "block the plate." The better athletes wanted no part of catching. They gravitated to the more glamourous positions—pitcher, short, centerfield—and took it from there.

And what did the catcher have? Well, he was immediately handed a mask; a big, cumbersome glove; a chest protector; and shin guards. Catcher's equipment. And what was this equipment called in baseball jargon? *The tools of ignorance.* The implication was clear. Anyone who was dumb enough to be a catcher deserved the tools of ignorance.

Then there were the physical risks involved in catching. It's a debilitating position. In an average nine-inning game the catcher must squat and rise an average of 200 times, a task so wearing on the legs that most catchers seem to get slower and slower as their careers progress.

And if this wasn't enough, there was always the threat of a foul tip splitting or breaking a finger, hand, or wrist. Catchers' hands were always bruised and battered, and they always played the game in some kind of pain.

Then there were the head-on collisions at home plate. The stationary catcher was always fair game for the base runner barreling in from third. How many times have you seen catchers knocked sprawling into the dust? A catcher takes the same kind of knocks that football players absorb, and if he fails to hold onto the ball, a ball park full of fans knows it immediately and shows its displeasure with boos.

There is a cute, yet apropos story involving the late, great heavyweight boxing champion, Rocky Marciano. When the Rock was a youngster he played baseball, and because of his build, he was a catcher. Finally the time came when Rocky had to choose between baseball and boxing. He chose boxing, and his mother breathed a sigh of relief. Said Mrs. Marciano:

"I didn't raise my son to be a catcher!"

No wonder. Who in his right mind would want to be a catcher? And to top it off, a catcher couldn't be a dummy. He has one of the most mentally taxing jobs on the field. After all, he must be aware of the game situation, more so than anyone else. He has to know the hitters and be able to tell his pitchers how to handle them. He's got to move his infielders and outfielders around and remind them of situations that might arise. He's also got to be an amateur psychologist, drawing every ounce of strength from his pitcher, and he must know immediately when that pitcher is losing his edge. If the catcher blows it, the whole game might be lost.

Thus, for many years from the late forties to the early sixties, there wasn't much beyond Berra and Campanella. Most of the others were slow-footed plodders, who were trained to handle the mitt adequately and were built to take the beating. Rarely did they contribute much with their bats. But that was an accepted part of the game then. 'If you had a catcher who could catch, that was blessing enough.

What changed the situation? For one thing, a

young catcher with the Chicago Cubs in the mid-1960s began doing something the old-time catchers wouldn't have dreamed of doing. He was Randy Hundley, and he introduced a one-handed style of catching. Using a flexible, deep-pocketed mitt, Hundley caught his pitcher with just his gloved hand, much like a first baseman does. When the pitch was delivered, he tucked his bare hand safely behind his body, and in one quick innovation eliminated the number-one hazard of catching, the split, sprained, bruised, and broken finger, which usually occurred on that exposed hand. Imagine a kid catcher in Little League, Babe Ruth League, or high school, splitting fingers every few games. Just how long is that kid going to stay a catcher? But as soon as Hundley's style became accepted (and it didn't take long), kids everywhere were following it.

Plus there was the old business maxim of supply and demand. The lack of good catchers received more publicity as media coverage of baseball increased in the fifties and sixties, and this gave coaches and even parents the idea of encouraging youngsters to catch.

"Listen, kid. There are plenty of pitchers and outfielders. But good catchers are hard to find. Become a good catcher and you've got a better shot at making the majors."

This philosophy, too, contributed to more youngsters sticking with the position throughout their growing years. But perhaps the final cog in the catching wheel was the arrival of a dynamic young catcher on the baseball scene in 1968. He was Johnny Bench of the Cincinnati Reds.

Bench came to the majors as a poised, confi-

dent, outgoing twenty-year-old, who took over the
Cincy catching job and handled it like a veteran.
Almost overnight, his baseball abilities and personality gave the position a new aura of glamour.
Bench seemed to be everywhere, in newspapers,
magazines, on television, interviewed here and
there, everywhere. And he produced. Catching
with Hundley's one-handed style, he was in-
stantly the best defensive catcher in the league.
He could throw like a bullet, hit with power, and
even run fairly well. And he was durable. He gave
other young catchers the incentive to stay with
the position instead of begging off, moving to first
base or the outfield.

It didn't take long for the catchers to follow
Bench and create a whole new breed behind the
plate. Pittsburgh's Manny Sanguillan, who caught
very well, was a top hitter, a free swinger like Clemente, but he also had the running speed of a
Maury Wills. Ted Simmons of the Cards was an
explosive switch hitter, another poised youngster
who did it all. Munson came up about the same
time, followed by Fisk, and there were other
youngsters right behind who also showed great
potential. Most of them could catch well, and in
the age of the base stealer, also throw. Yet unlike
some of their predecessors, they could also run
and hit. And the young ones keep coming.

And where does this leave Thurman Munson?
Undoubtedly near the top in ability, but somewhere else when it comes to charisma. Munson is
just not the kind of guy who stands out in a
crowd. Yet from the time he joined the Yanks in
1970, he has been marked for stardom.

Thurman Lee Munson was born on June 7,

1947, in Akron, Ohio. He grew up in nearby Canton, which is known as the home of Football's Hall of Fame. But Thurman's eye was on the Hall at Cooperstown.

It was a good childhood for Thurman, though his family didn't have much money. His father was a long-distance truck driver, so he was often away from home for days at a stretch. And as Thurman remembers:

"Truck drivers didn't make much money then, and it was really tough for him supporting a family of four kids. Yeah, we had food and clothing, all right, but not a dime left over after that."

Yet young Thurman admired his father and credits the elder Munson with giving him the attributes that later led to his success.

"My father was a go-getter," Thurm says. "I think he's the one who always made me want to play hard. He always wanted me to do better. I remember once he came to see me play in the minors. I had a great day at the plate—five for five, I think, with a couple of home runs. After the game what does my father tell me? He tells me I really looked bad behind the plate. That's the way he was. He wanted me to improve, so to my face he'd often criticize me, but to everybody else he'd say, 'Hey, that's my son.' So I always knew he was proud."

Thurm's brother Duane was also a fine athlete, but it was Thurman who had the extra incentive that led him to the majors. Thurman explains:

"Duane was a great athlete, but he didn't care that much whether he won or lost. I never could play that way. I've got to play hard. If you're that way, you don't leave yourself open to criticism.

And if I don't slide hard, I can't expect the other guys to do it."

So Thurm always had the makings of a leader. As a youngster he played various sports: baseball in the summer, football in the fall, and basketball during the winter. He became an outstanding player in all three, and when he reached high school, he became a star in each.

In football, he was a wingback on offense and a linebacker on defense. The hard contact got him ready for those future collisions at the plate. And as a wingback, he had to have speed. Thurman Munson isn't slow.

He wasn't slow on the basketball court, either. He couldn't be, because he played guard and averaged some twenty points per game. He was good enough on the hardwood to be selected for the All-County team his senior year.

That left baseball. There was never any doubt that baseball was Thurm's best sport, yet prior to his senior year in high school, he wasn't a catcher. He shied away from the position for the same reasons so many other youngsters did. He preferred to play shortstop, and he played both short and second base during his first two years. Then in his senior year, when the need arose, team-player Munson volunteered to move behind the plate.

He took to the position very quickly, surprising his coaches and teammates alike. And he enjoyed playing there, because he was really in the game and could lead from his backstop slot. The physical part didn't bother him, and once he mastered some of the other fundamentals, he was outstanding.

Despite his obvious baseball ability, Thurm

found himself flooded with scholarship offers to play college football. Football, of course, is a much more glamourous college sport than baseball, and there are many more recruiters shopping around with offers. Thurm was flattered, yet hesitant.

"I knew baseball was my best sport, and I wanted to continue at it. Even if I played college football and did well, I knew I'd never play in the pros. But I needed a scholarship to attend college, and I kept waiting."

Finally, the one he wanted came along. Kent State University in Ohio offered him a baseball scholarship and he grabbed it. By then he was committed to catching, and he immediately became an outstanding player at Kent State. He was also thinking of the major leagues by then. So he worked extra hard to attract attention. After all, Kent State wasn't exactly at the zenith of the college baseball world. The school isn't usually spoken of in the same breath as, say, Arizona State, or USC. But they played a good schedule and the scouts came.

Yet even then Thurm wasn't the flashy type. He often went unnoticed, as he did the little things that help win ball games. The fact that he still wasn't an outstanding hitter didn't help. He was good enough to become an All-America choice after the 1968 season, but it was his last year and he began to worry. What he didn't know at the time was that there was a scout watching him, watching him very closely.

The man was Gene Woodling, a name that should sound familiar to baseball fans. Woodling was a star outfielder with the New York Yankees

in the late forties and fifties, when the Yanks were
reeling off world championships like they were
duck soup. An outstanding hitter, Woodling contributed mightily to many a Yankee victory. Now
he was a chief scout for the Yanks, an important
job because the scouts are the men who keep the
talent rolling in.

There was a time when scouts had even more
power. Clubs entrusted these wily judges of talent to sign players right on the spot. The classic
story is that of veteran scout Tom Greenwade signing Mickey Mantle to a Yankee contract before
anyone in the Yankee organization even laid eyes
on him.

"It's not at all that way today," Gene Woodling
says. "Today we have the free-agent draft, where
teams choose players in order, much as they do in
football and basketball. And the team that picks
the player is the only one that can bid for his
services. If they can't reach an agreement, then
the player goes back into the pool and can be
drafted again.

"It's a good system in that it eliminates much of
the backbiting and lying that went on. A scout
can't make a boy false promises because the
parent club controls the draft. And this way, all
the scouts help each other and kind of work together. There's no way you can hide a good boy, so
you might as well let the other guy know about
him. He might help you by showing you a boy that
would better suit your club's needs."

Gene Woodling knew that the Yankees needed
a catcher in 1968. In fact, it was the first time in
many years that the club did not have a first-rate

backstop, which had been as much of a Yankee tradition as anything else.

The great Bill Dickey caught for the Bronx Bombers from 1928 to 1946, getting nearly 2,000 hits and compiling a life-time average of .313. Many consider him the greatest catcher of all time. Dickey retired as an active player in 1946, the same year that a youngster named Larry "Yogi" Berra came to the Yanks.

Yogi took over the number one job and held it right into the 1960s. Another Hall of Famer, Yogi blasted 358 home runs and was named the American League's Most Valuable Player three times. He is remembered as a fine catcher and one of the most dangerous clutch hitters of all time.

When Yogi retired in 1963, the Yanks already had his successor; in fact, Elston Howard had been splitting the job with Yogi for a number of seasons. Howard came to the majors later in baseball life than most, and didn't have as long a career as the other two. But he took over from Yogi and held the job until 1967. He, too, was an outstanding catcher and strong hitter, and he also took the American League's MVP prize one year.

So from 1928 until 1967, a period of forty years, the New York Yankees always had one of baseball's best catchers receiving for them. But there was no immediate replacement when Howard left, and several players shared the position for the next few seasons. That's why all the Yankee scouts were keeping especially alert for any bright young catching prospects. And Gene Woodling found one at Kent State in 1968.

What does a scout look for in a player? Gene

talked about that and about which of those qualities he saw in young Thurman Munson:

"First of all, we have to look at a lot of ballplayers, so we've got to be able to evaluate a boy
quickly. My territory, for instance, consists of all
of Ohio and Michigan, and parts of Kentucky and
Indiana. I have two other men working for me
and the three of us have to cover everything in
these states. When you think that there are some
sixty-eight colleges playing baseball in Ohio
alone, you begin to get the total picture. We not
only cover colleges, but also high schools, Legion
games and any other leads that might come in.
It's a mammoth job."

The first thing Gene Woodling looks at when
he's scouting a youngster is the boy's speed and
his arm:

"These two things are a must for a major
leaguer. No way a guy is going to make it if he
has minimal throwing skills and little speed. Some
guys also look at size. I don't. A kid of 5'-8" or
5'-9" can certainly play big league ball.

"So what I'm looking for are basic tools. I know
you're probably wondering why I didn't mention
hitting. I have a reason. There's just no way you
can figure out that bat. I played major league ball
for almost twenty years, and I never figured it
out. A kid can hit a ton in high school or college,
then he runs into curves, sliders, the whole bit,
and comes up empty."

What was Gene's first reaction when he saw
Thurman Munson at Kent State?

"The first thing I noticed about Thurman was
his speed," recalls Gene. "He was exceptionally
fast for a catcher. As you know, catchers can

sometimes get away with being rather slow, but this kid could run.

"Then I noticed his arm. It was strong, not the strongest I'd ever seen, but strong enough. The thing about it was the quickness. Thurm had, and still has, the quickest arm I've ever seen on a catcher, and I think he's proved it in the big leagues. Anyway, when I saw him throw I was just about convinced."

So those were the basics that Gene Woodling looked for. He liked what he saw that first time, then tried to see a bit more when he returned, for he already had Munson high on his list of possibilities:

"As I watched him some more, I could see that he already had outstanding ability as a catcher. In other words, defensively, he was major league caliber. He stood out like a light bulb with those guys he was playing with.

"His hitting was just so-so. In fact, I had some reservations about it, but as I said, that's the last thing I worry about. In fact, I'll admit now that Thurm's hit a lot better than I thought he would since he's been in the majors. Anyway, it didn't take long for me to decide he was the real goods."

Unlike some scouts, Gene didn't rush up to Munson, introduce himself, and try to sell the youngster a bill of goods. Instead he simply submitted Thurm's name to the Yankee office with his recommendation and let them take it from there.

"There were a large number of scouts around Thurman that year," Gene remembers, "yet I never met him in person. I'd rather not let a boy know I'm there watching him. That way, he'll just

play naturally. Once the Yanks picked Thurman,
I went back in, introduced myself, and did the
actual signing."

Perhaps because of his childhood, Thurman
was highly motivated by money. Oh, sure, he had
a driving desire to excel and win, but he also
wanted to be compensated for it. He signed with
the Yanks for a modest bonus, as much as he
thought he was worth then, and immediately
went about the business of making the big
leagues—but not before he began juggling his
money.

"I was always interested in money," Thurm admitted. "But when I first signed, got my bonus,
and saw how much tax they took out of it, I said,
'My God, if they're gonna do this to me—if I ever
really start making some money, I'm gonna be in
trouble. So I took the little money I had left after
taxes and put it into real estate."

Thurm's salary has, of course, moved into the
upper brackets, but he still invests carefully,
hoping to lay the groundwork for a going business
when he retires.

But back to baseball. After signing Munson, the
Yanks immediately sent him to Binghamton, New
York, where he played in seventy-one games before the 1968 season ended. But he was impressive, catching very well and hitting .301, with
68 hits in 226 at bats. He had six homers and 37
RBI's. At age twenty-one, he seemed to be pro-
gressing rapidly. That was good news, because
the Yanks needed him.

By now, everyone knows the story of the New
York Yankees, and how they dominated the game
of baseball for nearly four and one-half decades,

from the early 1920s to the mid-1960s. Between 1921 and 1964, the Yankees won 29 American League pennants and 20 world championships, a record miles ahead of any other team.

From 1949 to 1964, the club took 14 pennants in 16 years, an amazing achievement, winning 5 in a row twice and 4 straight once. And the first 5, from 1949 to 1953, resulted in 5 consecutive world titles. They were the supreme dynasty in all of sports.

But after the 1964 season the team suddenly fell apart. Veteran stars like Mantle, Maris, Ford, Pepitone, Boyer, and Tresh all seemed to go at once—some to age, some prematurely. But they stopped producing at the same time and in the space of a single season the club nosedived from first to sixth. A year later, in 1966, they fell to tenth and were last in the American League. They were ninth the year after that, then seemed to level off and play around the .500 mark in 1968 and 1969. But it wasn't the same.

In 1969, Thurman was sent to Syracuse, the Yanks' top farm team in the International League. He played just twenty-eight games there, starring with a .363 batting average and catching extremely well. Then the Yanks called him to the Bronx and the big club. He had played just ninety-nine games in the minors, and he was never to return. When someone asked Thurm why he worked so hard to get to the majors he gave a typical answer:

"You don't get rich playing in Syracuse."

But it was also pride and desire. Thurm felt he was ready, and he was happy to get the call. He spent the remainder of the 1969 season as a backup for veteran Jake Gibbs. Though he played in just twenty-six games, he did well, batting .256 on 22 for 86, hitting his first homer, and driving in nine runs. His poise and ability behind the plate surprised everyone as well.

So when spring training for 1970 rolled around, the Yanks decided to give Thurman a real shot at the starting job. The veteran Gibbs was still there, but they knew what he could do. Another youngster, John Ellis, was also in the sweepstakes.

As the exhibition season unfolded, both Munson and Ellis were hitting a ton; both were well over .300 and looked extremely good. The difference was that Thurman was a much more accomplished catcher at that time. Ellis, though big and strong, did not have Thurm's skills behind the plate. So toward the end of the practice games, Ellis was moved to first base. Both rookies had won jobs and the Yanks were excited about the upcoming season.

Before opening day, Thurm was talking about his chances for a strong rookie year, and he was already mentioning the fact that he didn't have classic form:

"I don't see why I shouldn't have a good year. I've been preparing for this for a long time, working hard toward it, and I feel I'm ready. I know there are people who don't agree with me. I remember when I was at Kent State and the scouts were beginning to come. There was one guy, from the Cleveland Indians, who said I couldn't run, said I couldn't play in the big leagues. I don't know who he was looking at because I could run in high school. I was fast. But that's just what I mean about not looking good when I do things."

So the Yanks opened the 1970 season with some new faces in the lineup. Yet in a matter of weeks, the new faces seemed destined to disappear. Both Thurm and Ellis, the hottest hitters in the spring, were suddenly cool when the real thing started. Each was struggling, and fans began to wonder if they were just spring phenoms, the kind that cause all sorts of excitement, then fizzle out just as quickly, never to be seen again.

For awhile it seemed as if Thurman Munson might fit into that category. After his first 30 at bats of 1970, Thurm had just one hit! One hit in 30 at bats! That's a batting average of .033. Reporters were already beginning to stay away from the youngster, figuring he'd have nothing to say, and also figuring he wouldn't be around much longer. But one brave soul ventured up to Thurm and asked him if he thought he could pull his game together. The answer he got was surprising.

"Don't worry about me," Thurm said. "When this year is over I'll be hitting .300."

The reporter couldn't believe it. Neither could anyone else. Here was this raw rookie, off to a horrendous start at the plate, still having the gumption to predict a .300 season. Some people laughed, the serious ones tried to show how difficult it would be for a player to pick up the slack from a start like that.

"He could get 25 hits in his next 70 at bats," said one, "and that's a .357 clip in itself. Yet it would just give him a .260 mark for his first 100 at bats of the season. It's a long way to come."

The thing that kept Thurman in the lineup was

his glove, his ability to handle the pitchers and
the game behind the plate. He caught with the
poise of a veteran, and he made even the older
pitchers feel comfortable working to him.

"He gives you a lot of confidence out there,"
said one veteran. "You start pitching to him, and
you forget he's just twenty-three years old."

Another said, "I remember reading stories
about Bench, how he bawled out veteran pitchers
his first year. This kid is the same way. If he feels
you're not putting out, or not doing something
right, he lets you know about it in no uncertain
terms. He's not afraid to speak out."

It was just a question of how long the Yanks
could put up with Munson's anemic bat. They
were already beginning to platoon Ellis at first.
His start had been almost as horrible as Thurm's.
Could the benching of Munson be far behind?

It's doubtful that the Yanks would have waited
much longer. But they didn't have to. Thurman finally began to hit. And he began to hit well.
From that point on, he was to hold up both ends
of his job.

As the year wore on, it became obvious that
Thurman's hitting was solid and steady. No more
bad slumps. And the Yanks were having a good
year. They were trailing powerful Baltimore but
were playing well over .500 ball and showing
signs of revival. They never did catch the Orioles,
but they finished the year with a 93-69 mark,
good for second place in the Eastern Division of
the American League.

And Thurman Munson had given the Yanks
even more than they hoped for. Amazingly, he
had made good his promise, hitting .302 (a club-

leading figure) for the season and .312 after that disastrous start. He played in 132 games and got 137 hits, including 6 homers and 53 RBI's. He was also outstanding behind the plate, working well with his pitchers and exhibiting that quick throwing arm that Gene Woodling had talked about. Base runners didn't take too many liberties with Thurman Munson back there.

It wasn't until several weeks after the season ended that Thurm really got the good news. He had been named American League Rookie of the Year for 1970.

But the next season, both Thurm and the Yankees fell back. The team barely played .500 ball, while Munson, off to another excruciatingly slow start, didn't recover quite as rapidly, finishing at just .251 with 10 homers and 42 RBI's in 125 games.

The only plus was his catching. There was little doubt now that he was one of the best receivers in baseball. It was his catching skills that got him selected to the All-Star team for the first time, and when the year ended he had some noteworthy catching stats.

Thurman led all major league receivers, including Bench, with a .998 fielding mark. He had committed just a single error in 615 chances, tying a Yankee catching mark held by Elston Howard. He had also thrown out 23 of the 38 runners who tried to steal on him. And far fewer were running on him than in his rookie season when they were all anxious to test him. There didn't seem to be any way to stop him from becoming the next catching star in the American League.

Then in 1972, another young catcher burst upon the A.L. He was Carlton Fisk of the Boston Red Sox, and without any advance notice, he began to take the league by storm. Playing in ancient Fenway Park with its short left-field wall, Fisk took advantage of the "Green Monster" and began hitting shots over it. Not that he didn't have power. Fisk was big and strong, a striking figure on the field, and this helped him attract new legions of fans. Ironically, his nickname was "Pudge," a name tagged on him years earlier, when he was heavier. Now, however, he symbolized to Thurman Munson, the typical long, lean, good-looking athlete. Munson thought of himself more as "pudge."

It wasn't that Fisk was having a better year than Munson. He wasn't, though he was producing more runs via the homer and RBI route. But the Yanks were faltering while the Sox were in a pennant race. And in August, Fisk's name hit the baseball world when, as a rookie, he publicly criticized such veterans as Carl Yastrzemski and Reggie Smith for not hustling.

All kinds of stories hit the wires on the young catcher, and his picture made the cover of national sports magazines, with titles such as "The Rookie Who Roused the Red Sox." Some writer mentioned that the handsome Fisk looked a lot like movie star Charlton Heston. And so forth. So by the time the 1972 season ended, it was Carlton Fisk, not Thurman Munson, who was the American League's answer to Johnny Bench. And a rivalry was born between the two that continues to this day.

There wasn't a whole lot to choose from in the

stats. Thurman had a good year, both at the plate and in the field. He upped his average to .280, hitting 7 homers and drove home 46 runs; while Fisk hit .293, with 22 homers and 61 RBI's. Fisk's bat had certainly been more productive, but Thurman had been a .300 hitter as a rookie. Then, like Munson before him, Fisk was named American League Rookie of the Year.

Thurm's image troubles really started during 1973. He was having a good year at the plate, his best ever, since his power production was up and his batting average around the .300 mark. Fisk, in the meantime, was still hitting homers over the wall in Boston, but his average was hovering around the .250 mark. And while Fisk was good defensively, there really weren't too many people who would claim he was better than Munson. Yet Fisk was more of a holler guy, more vocal, and thus his name was always in the papers. As they say in the press, he was "good copy."

That's undoubtedly part of the reason that Fisk beat out Munson for the starting berth on the All-Star team. But when he beat him out by some half million votes, Munson really fumed; he couldn't keep quiet about it any longer.

Finally, he popped off to a reporter. "I'm not taking anything away from Fisk," said Munson, "but get him away from Fenway Park and that easy wall in left field and see how many home runs he hits."

Not one to take those matters lightly, Fisk responded to the challenge:

"I don't want to bad-mouth Munson," said Carlton, "but he is jealous of me. He wants to be the American League All-Star catcher, but I took it away from him. He always wants to talk when he comes to bat. He must think he's another Yogi Berra, which he isn't."

Bang! Just like that there was a feud. And when there's a hint of a feud in the air reporters come around. Suddenly, more of them than ever wanted to talk with Thurman Munson, and before long the discussion would come down to a matter of Fisk and recognition.

"Everybody wants recognition," Thurm said. "And the best way to get recognition is to hit forty home runs or win twenty games as a pitcher. I'm a line drive hitter, so the best way for me to get recognition is to have the Yankees get into the world series."

But Thurm admitted that he felt image also had something to do with it, and in that respect, he wasn't the perfect example of the classic catcher.

"I don't throw the ball as hard as some catchers," he said, "but I get it where I want it to go. I'm squatty, I have a big hind end, and I say what I think. But I'll tell you something. I bet if you ask Ralph [Yankee manager Ralph Houk] if he'd trade me one-on-one with anyone, there'd be only one person he'd do it for, and that would be Johnny Bench."

The All-Star Game came and went, with Munson serving as backup for starter Fisk. But the harsh words of the earlier time weren't forgotten. And on August 1, 1973, the whole thing boiled over.

The Yanks were playing the Red Sox up at Fenway. Both were still in the pennant race and it was a hard-fought game, as most Yankee-Red Sox games are. It was tied at 2-2 in the ninth inning; Yanks up.

Munson was batting against Red Sox lefthander John Curtis, and he promptly rapped a hard double to left. When Graig Nettles grounded out, Munson ran to third. Now Felipe Alou was up. He was walked intentionally, bringing up shortstop Gene Michael. That's when Manager Houk called for a suicide squeeze.

The suicide squeeze is one of baseball's most exciting plays. As the pitcher winds up, the runner on third breaks for home. It's then up to the batter to bunt the ball—almost anywhere—because if he gets his bat on it, the breaking runner will almost always make it. But if he misses, then there's a play at the plate with the odds against the runner. It's exciting because the play is committed from the time the runner breaks. Even if the pitch is in the dirt, the batter must go after it, because the runner has usually passed the point of no return.

So Munson was coming hard. Curtis threw a low outside curve that Michael had to lunge for. He missed. Thurm could have stopped, but instead he kept on running. He barreled into Fisk full force and the two went rolling on the ground. Thurman got up swinging. Without hesitating, Fisk swung back.

When Fisk's fist grazed Michael, who was still in the box, he jumped into the fray. Players from both dugouts rushed onto the field as Munson and Fisk were still trying to get at each other. Finally a couple of Red Sox got Munson and pinned him to the ground, thus ending the brawl.

But it didn't end for Thurm. He was still angry

when reporters asked him about the incident several days later.

"I weigh 190 pounds," he said. "I'm no Lou Brock. What good would it have done me to get caught in a rundown. So I ran over Fisk. I just felt that he kicked me off him when I did it. He said the next day, in the papers, that the reason he kicked me off was so that he could get up and throw. Well, fine. But at the time, that explanation didn't satisfy me. So I got up and hit him."

There's generally no winner and loser in baseball fights. They end up as hapless wrestling matches with a lot of guys pushing and shoving. But witnesses say Fisk had a cut under his right eye and one on the chin. Munson was unmarked, and even managed to see something positive in the whole thing.

"For me, the hassle with Fisk turned into a lot of national press," he said. "Even being notorious is better than being ignored."

In a way, Thurm was right. The brawl with Fisk got him more press than usual and brought to light their rivalry for American League catching supremacy. As a consequence, more people than ever watched the two during the second half of the 1973 season. And the turn of events in that last few months of the year must have pleased Thurm very much.

He continued to wield a hot bat, while Fisk faltered. In fact, many fans began to look at Thurm in a different light. He was seen as a kind of leader on the Yanks, a silent leader who let his deeds on the diamond, not his mouth, do the talking for him.

He was also being looked upon more and more

as the good guy in the Boston brawl, not so much because of anything he did, but because Carlton Fisk seemed to be in another melee each week. First there was a home plate brawl with Al Gallagher of the Angels. Then another Angel, Bob Oliver, had to be restrained from going after Fisk by five teammates. In addition, Fisk almost came to blows with veteran outfield great Frank Robinson. There were quotes floating around the league that Fisk was becoming too big for his britches.

Thurm was probably more contented with himself than ever before in the final months of the 1973 season. He sensed a measure of vindication for the All-Star snub, and he knew he was completing his finest season. The one problem was that the Yanks had again dropped out of the pennant race. The team wasn't strong enough to make a real run at it.

At the end, Thurm had hit .301, with 20 home runs and 74 RBI's (both career highs for him). He had 156 hits in 519 at bats. Fisk, by contrast, had just 125 hits in 508 at bats. He hit more homers than Thurm, getting 26, but drove in just 71 runs and batted .246. The edge had to go to Munson.

While Thurman Munson still wasn't a household name across America, the respect for the solid catcher was enormous among members of the Yankee family. Before the 1974 season started, ex-ballplayer turned Yankee sportscaster, Bill White, talked about Munson and his talents.

"Bench is the only catcher in either league who might be better than Munson right now," said Bill. "Anybody like Thurm, who uses the whole field to hit is a good hitter. Look at the guys who consistently hit .300—Aaron, Rose, Carew—they hit the ball all over. Munson does that. He can hit the ball to right field, he can hit and run for you."

New Yankee manager Bill Virdon, who took over for Ralph Houk during the 1973 season, loved the catcher he inherited with the job.

"If I had twenty-five guys like Thurman Munson, I wouldn't even have to manage this team," said Virdon. "He does everything well. He's aggressive. He's not as big as some good ones I've seen, but he's strong and quick. There's also a lot of enthusiasm in him. His only defect may be that sometimes he throws a little too enthusiastically."

Bill White agreed with that:

"Sometimes it seems that Thurm wants to gun that guy down at second by fifteen yards instead of getting him by three or four feet. When that happens, he ends up throwing the ball into centerfield. But as for the strength of his arm, let's face it, to be a catcher you don't have to have that much of a gun. Thurm is quick. I've been in baseball a long time, and I have yet to see anybody outrun a baseball."

Rushing some throws was just an outgrowth of Thurm's overall desire and enthusiasm. He's always played hard. It was just a matter of getting his game under a bit more control.

When 1974 started it looked like a promising year for both Thurm and the Yanks. The team was hanging close to the American League lead, and Munson was off to a pretty good start, which for him, a notoriously slow starter, was a blessing. In addition, Munson's rival, Fisk, was on the shelf with a serious knee injury that required surgery. Munson would have the field to himself.

Then it happened. It was still early in the season when a left-handed batter took a big riff at the ball and missed. His backswing came way back and caught Munson on his right hand. It was a painful injury and Thurm was taken to the hospital for X-rays. Fortunately, they were negative—no broken bones, just a very bad bruise. The hand really pained Thurm, but the Yanks were finally in a pennant race and he didn't want to stay out of the lineup. So he begged in, and Manager Virdon gave him the green light. With a pennant race on and no broken bones in the hand, no way Thurm was going to stay out of that lineup a day longer than was absolutely necessary.

But he should have. Getting back in there too soon caused other problems, both in the field and at the bat. Since his hand still hadn't healed properly, Munson was forced to grip both ball and bat differently. He couldn't swing well either, and his average dropped off. Behind the plate the altered grip didn't make for good throwing, so Thurm tried to compensate. He began throwing another way and came up with elbow problems. And the hand couldn't complete the healing process because it was always being aggravated by catching or swinging the bat. The injury lingered, and it affected Thurm's play.

Yet he hung in there, right to the end, as the Yanks stayed in the pennant race right up until the final weekend of the season, losing out by a mere two games. Thurm's stats weren't bad, but in view of the '73 season, he felt they were disappointing. He finished with a .261 average, 13 homers, and 60 RBI's.

"I definitely would have had better numbers if

it wasn't for the hand. I'm not trying to make excuses, but I really couldn't grip the bat properly and my whole defensive game was hurting. It's disappointing to me because I felt I could have helped the club a lot more. Maybe if I didn't hurt the hand we would have come out on top."

As usual, Thurm was thinking of the team first. But the Yanks had done well, especially since they hadn't even been in their home park. The legendary Yankee Stadium was being renovated, modernized so it could compete with the newer parks in the league. The Yanks played all their home games in 1974 at Shea Stadium, the home of the National League Mets. They'd be playing at Shea again in 1975, before returning to their own park in 1976.

And by now the Yankee brass was getting pennant hungry. The team hadn't won since 1964, by far the longest winless stretch since that first flag in 1921. So during the off-season they began to make some big moves.

First of all, there was a major trade with the San Francisco Giants. The Yanks gave up their big star, Bobby Murcer, who was supposed to be the next DiMaggio or Mantle. But Bobby, a good ballplayer, always played in the shadows of those two greats. He wasn't the power hitter they were, though he often tried to be. And when he was moved from centerfield to right, to make room for the slick fielding Elliott Maddox, he began to sulk. A change had to be made.

In return for Murcer, the Yanks got Bobby Bonds, one of the most exciting players in the major leagues. The speedy Bonds was a powerhouse, a player who could do it all, having a career high of 39 homers. He was also capable of stealing more than 50 bases a year and often batted leadoff for the Giants. But Bonds, too, played in a shadow. He was always expected to be the next Willie Mays, and those shoes are too big for any man to fill. So the trade was looked upon as beneficial to both teams.

Then the Yanks really pulled a coup. The Oakland A's superpitcher, Jim "Catfish" Hunter, won a court battle against team owner Charles O. Finley and was declared a free agent. Teams in both leagues bid for Catfish's services, and the Yankees won, with something like a $3.75 million offer for five years.

With Bonds and Hunter added to a roster that already included Thurm Munson, Roy White, Elliott Maddox, Graig Nettles, Lou Pinella, Ron Blomberg, and others, the Yanks were suddenly favorites to take the A.L. flag. The pressure was on.

The Yanks got off the mark fairly well, keeping within striking distance of the top. But it wasn't Hunter or Bonds who led the early-season surge. It was Munson, who was off to the best start of his career. The hand seemed well again, and Thurm was hitting well over .300. Manager Virdon installed him in the fourth spot in the order, the clean-up spot, and he continued to do the job.

In his own way, he was also becoming the team leader. In fact, word began drifting out of the Yankee organization that Munson was now "the soul of the team," that he was "the one player the Yankees could least afford to lose." Thurm was valuable, all right.

The story also came out that Munson was in-

strumental in the Yankees' signing of Hunter, that
he called Catfish several times during the negotia-
tion period to persuade him to accept the Yanks'
offer.

And it was Thurman Munson who became
Bobby Bonds' biggest booster when Bonds was in
an early-season slump. Thurman constantly worked
at settling Bobby down, trying to ease the
pressure and reminding him that "we all know
you can hit." And slowly, Bonds began coming
out of it. In fact, he went on a tear and jumped to
the top of the league in homers and RBI's. And
by the end of May, the Yanks had also jumped to
the top of their division.

Naturally, it was Bonds and the fast-recovering
Hunter who were getting the publicity. There was
also much talk about the contributions of Roy
White and Elliott Maddox, both of whom went on
early-season batting tears. Then Graig Nettles
took off on one of his patented hitting sprees.
Once again, not much notice came to Munson,
who was still way over .300 and playing steady
ball. It bugged him again. One writer called him
the "tormented all-star." And he still chafed when
someone mentioned Carlton Fisk. Oddly enough,
Fisk, who had missed almost all of 1974 with a
knee injury, was on the disabled list again, this
time with a broken arm. But it didn't stop Thurm
from sounding off when someone mentioned Fisk.

"Compared to him, why should I be so over-
looked," he said. "He's a good ballplayer, but I
don't think he's much of a threat in other parks as
he is in Boston; he might be a better ballplayer
than I am, but he has never done the things I've
done—set a defensive record for catchers, set a

record for assists, hit .300 twice. And in six and a half years in the big leagues, how many games have I missed?

"I know I run better than him, and I know nobody plays harder than I do. Now Johnny Bench is different. I've never hit 40 home runs or driven in 120 runs. I haven't done those things. So I can't talk about me being as good as Bench because I haven't done what he's done.

"Sometimes I wonder why playing hard hasn't helped my image. But it hasn't. Pete Rose plays that way. Charlie Hustle they call him. He gets more recognition for hustling than he does for playing the game, and he's a great player. I've always played hard. I thought that's the way you were supposed to play."

It might have sounded like sour grapes to some, but Munson was just being honest, saying the things that were on his mind. Maybe he's harped on the recognition bit for a long time, but when a player is as good as Thurm, he has the right.

Anyway, the Yankees were going real well into June when disaster struck. First Maddox went out with a knee injury that finished him for the year. One of the best defensive outfielders in the business and a .300 hitter, he had been the glue that held the outfield together. And shortly after that, Bonds hurt a knee. The injury was not bad enough to keep Bonds out, but like Munson's hand injury of the year before, it hampered his performance for the rest of the season.

After that it seemed like a jinx. Hard-hitting Ron Blomberg threw his shoulder out and kissed the season goodbye. Outfielder Lou Pinella suffered a mysterious inner ear problem that required corrective surgery. Pitchers Doc Medich, Pat Dobson, and Sparky Lyle all performed at levels below their best. In effect, a good portion of the team was either hurt or slumping. The team suddenly dropped right out of the race.

Almost everyone was affected by the team slump—except Thurman Munson. He was playing his heart out, staying up among the league leaders in hitting and RBI's. He was the starting All-Star catcher by a large margin (Fisk was still injured), and people began saying he had a good shot at the league's MVP prize.

Thurm's pace never slowed, but the Yankees never picked up. Near the end of the year Manager Virdon was fired, and he was replaced by the volatile Billy Martin, an ex-Yankee, whose thoughts immediately turned to next year. And in August, team president Gabe Paul admitted the season had been very disappointing to him.

"There have been ups and downs in my baseball life," Paul said, "but this year has been very frustrating for us. We all expected better. The whole country expected better."

So the season was a real downer. And it was a shame, since Thurman Munson had the greatest season of his career. He came to bat 597 times, collecting 190 hits for a .318 average, third best in the league. Though he hit just 12 homers, he nevertheless became the first Yankee since 1964 to drive in more than 100 runs, finishing with 102. Had the Yankees been in the pennant race, or won it, most experts feel that Thurm would have indeed been the league's MVP. He was certainly the most valuable member of the Yankees.

"My hand didn't hurt at all this year," said

Thurm, "but it still wasn't as strong as I would have liked. I think I could have hit more home runs if it had been stronger. I wasn't getting that extra ten feet that can mean the difference between a homer and a drive to the wall."

Ironically, when his greatest season ended, Thurm Munson found himself still haunted by the specter of Carlton Fisk. Fisk returned to the Red Sox lineup in the second half of the season and played brilliantly. Though he didn't qualify for the batting race, he hit .331, with 10 homers and 52 RBI's in an abbreviated season. And he helped his team win the American League pennant. Fisk was then a central figure in the world series, hitting a pair of homers, one of which (coming in extra innings) tied the series in game six. Experts call that game one of the greatest ever played.

Even though the Cincinnati Reds won the series in seven games, the Sox came out of it as something akin to folk heroes. And in the minds of many who watched, Carlton Fisk is still the best catcher in the American League and the other guy is still Thurman Who?

Maybe it will always be that way. And maybe Thurman Munson will always be tormented by it. But he's still young and his best years should still be ahead of him. It will be very interesting to watch the Munson-Fisk rivalry in upcoming seasons.

As for Thurman, he's never lost his zest for the game or for winning. The Yankees will return to their own ball park in 1976, and they hope to create their own Bicentennial celebration. Thurman is already looking forward to that.

"I'll be better next year," he said. "I'll be ready
for Yankee Stadium again. Maybe I'll be a switch
hitter."

The reporters blinked. Thurman, a switch hitter?

"Sure, I used to fool around a lot hitting left-
handed, but it always hurt my right elbow when I
swung, so I don't know how serious I am about it."

But Thurman Munson's next comment was serious, as well as typical of the man and the ballplayer.

"I really don't think about personal honors,"
Thurm said. "I just want to have a good finish
and win everything next year."

If the Yankees do win it all, next year or the
year after or the year after that, one thing is for
sure. Thurman Munson will play a major role in
winning. He has always been a winner, and he's
carrying on in a great winning tradition. The
Yankee catcher fully deserves his place among the
great line of men who preceded him. They'll all
be remembered—Dickey, Berra, Howard, and
Thurm Munson, winners all.

Steve Garvey

In a sense, it's all too perfect. But then again, it's all true, and you can't change that. If they decide to make a movie out of it, the title is a natural: *Born to Be a Dodger*. The subtitle? *The Steve Garvey Story*.

It's the way stories used to be: young boy becomes team bat boy; idolizes popular, clean-cut first baseman; pursues own career; winds up playing first base for the same team; becomes star and Most Valuable Player, then tells reporters:

"I sincerely think I was born to be a Dodger."

Fade out. The perfect ending—unless you want to show the hero jogging into the sunset, glove and bat in hand, with the doors of the Hall of Fame opening wide to greet him. That part of the story hasn't been played out yet, but the way Steve Garvey has been going, can the story end any other way?

Steve Garvey, of course, is the first baseman for the Los Angeles Dodgers, a man who, in 1974 and 1975, put together two of the most consistently outstanding seasons in recent years. And during that time, Steve has acquired a reputation as baseball's all-American boy, a positive thinking

41

athlete who feels very strongly about the ideals and responsibilities that go with being a professional ballplayer.

You get an idea of how Steve Garvey thinks when you hear him talk about his team.

"The Dodgers are a first-class organization," Steve has said. "Everyone is treated as if he is a member of the family, and I think that's the way it should be done.

"The team tries to draft players and develop them together in the minor leagues until they're ready to play together in the majors. There's a solid group of us who came up together on the team right now. And with players developed this way, instead of being thown together through trades, I think you get a more positive-thinking situation; the players feel they really belong. It's a kind of ... 'I grew up with these guys, we've played together as a unit' ... that kind of thing.

"We always travel first class in our own jet, stay at the finest places, play in the finest stadiums. It's a wonderful blend. You stand back, draw all the pieces together and you couldn't play for a finer group of people."

Because of his allegiance to his team and to the sport, Garvey feels he has a public obligation all year round.

"I try to go through life with the idea that maybe a little boy or girl is looking over my shoulder, following me around. I wouldn't want to do anything physically or vocally that would take away from their growing up. I try to be a positive image. I think that's the big thing."

Thus Steve Garvey has become the new Frank Merriwell, a superstar who does it all by the book,

the complete opposite of the so-called sports
"anti-hero," the athlete who does things his own
way and doesn't care who knows. Steve Garvey
doesn't dig them, and they don't dig Steve Garvey. In fact, there were stories coming from the
Dodger family in 1975 that had some teammates
publicly criticizing Steve's goodie-goodie role and
claiming he was trying to push his philosophy
onto them.

It was a ticklish situation, spurred perhaps by
the fact that the Dodgers, expected to retain the
National League championship they'd won in
1974, were hopelessly behind the Cincinnati
Reds by midseason. To a degree, the whispers
and the open statements that followed disillusioned Garvey, but he responded by playing even
harder on the field and acknowledging that he
wasn't about to change his ways because of the
feelings of other people.

But whether you think of Steve Garvey as an
all-American boy or as a guy whose hair is too
neat and whose views are too straight, you've still
got to admit two things. One is that he is an individual, a strong personality who expresses his
feelings and does his own thing. The other is that
Steve Garvey can play ball.

Compactly built at 5'-10", 195-pounds, Garvey is a smart, line-drive hitter who can spray the
ball to all fields. Since establishing himself as an
everyday player in 1974, he has proved day-in
and day-out that he's for real. In the past two seasons (1974 and 1975), he has shown enough
power to crack out 39 homers, collect 410 hits,
knock in 206 runs, and compile batting averages
of .312 and .319. His batting consistency has

been remarkable; and he's been just as consistent
in the field. Quickly becoming an outstanding first
baseman, Garvey made just eight errors in 1974
and eight more in '75.

Garvey's approach to the game is a cerebral
one; that is, he uses his head. During the 1974
World Series, for instance, the Oakland A's pitchers were constantly keeping the ball away from
the Dodger hitters. Most of the L.A. batters took
up the challenge and continued to try to pull and
as a consequence, floundered badly. Not Garvey.
He saw what was happening and quickly adjust-
ed his short, compact swing. The result was eight
hits, more than any other player on either team,
and a .381 batting average in five games.

Steve Garvey has been a winner for a long time.
In fact, listing his achievements from Little
League days on makes it look as if things always
came easy. But he had to work, and for a while, it
even looked as if he was destined to be nothing
more than a major league utility player. But once
given the opportunity, Steve Garvey made the
most of it.

Garvey was born on December 22, 1948, in
Tampa, Florida. His full name, Steven Patrick
Garvey, bespeaks his Irish origins. His family was
always a close-knit one, and his parents had a lot
of pride in their only child. Steve's father, Joe
Garvey was a good athlete. He had been a first
baseman on local and semi-pro teams and had
played some minor league football on Long Island
before the family moved to Tampa. Even Steve's
mother, Mildred, was athletic, having played a
great deal of field hockey as a youngster.

Mildred Garvey remembers kidding with Steve

because she was always more limber than he was. "He'd get mad at me because he couldn't get his foot up on this counter we had," she recalls. "I'd ask him to put his foot up on the counter like mine was, and he couldn't do it."

Steve's childhood was happy. Both his parents were easygoing and affable. There was a lot of laughter in the Garvey household. Steve played ball with his father and friends from an early age, and he soon found he was in the right place for a prospective ballplayer. Florida was the training ground for most of the major league teams, and there were always spring exhibition games going on in Tampa. Steve's father was a driver for the Greyhound Company and often transported the teams out to the ball park. He sometimes took young Steve along and pretty soon Steve was serving as a bat boy for several clubs, including the Dodgers, Yankees, and Tigers. It wasn't long before the Dodgers were his favorites.

In those days the Dodgers were a national league power. The team had dominated the National League in the early-to-mid-1950s, when it was located in Brooklyn. In fact, they were still the Brooklyn Dodgers when Steve first met them; they moved to Los Angeles before the 1958 season, when Steve was just nine.

The Dodgers had many stars then—Robinson, Hodges, Snider, Campanella, Furillo, Reese, Newcombe, Gilliam, Cox. They were almost household names, especially after they finally won their first world series in 1955. It was almost inevitable that the Dodgers would be Steve's favorites, and

that Gil Hodges would be his favorite person.
Steve remembers those days well.

"Gil Hodges was a gentleman on and off the
field. I always admired him. He always took time
to play catch with me or say a kind word. And his
handshake is something I'll never forget.

"There were all kinds of good memories of the
Dodgers, like the time they were playing in
Bradenton [Florida], and Carl Furillo was in
right field in water up to his ankles. He couldn't
have enjoyed it, but he stayed in there. I just had
the feeling that the Dodgers were a fine bunch of
men playing with a fine team, and they never did
anything to change that image.

"I was bat boy for the Yankees and Tigers to
some degree, too, but a few of the players on the
Yankees weren't quite what I expected. When you
have an idol, you always expect they're perfect.
You hear them say a few cuss words, or see them
refuse to sign a few autographs, and it takes some
of the shine off."

So even as a young boy, Steve had a good idea
how a professional athlete should be, and he ap-
parently saw more of these qualities in the
Dodgers than in any other team with which he
was associated.

Steve wasn't only a spectator then. At about the
same time as he became a bat boy, he also became a Little League star. His final Little League
season saw him hit .750, with 18 home runs in
20 games. That's three hits in every four trips to
the plate. Then Steve moved on to the Pony
League. In the first four innings of his very first
game he hit for the cycle (single, double, triple,

home run). Steve remembers how little things like that were always happening to him.

"It all began to add up and make me think, 'Maybe I am destined to be a professional athlete.'"

He was certainly thinking in terms of the major leagues:

"We had about eleven grapefruit trees in our backyard, and in the spring I'd take the little hard grapefruits that had fallen off and hit them with a broomstick. I'd pretend I was the Dodgers, and I'd imitate all their players. I remember even hitting line drives back then, with the grapefruits."

Much of the credit for Steve's hitting success is his compact build, which allows for that quick, short, compact hitting stroke. And much of the strength in the stroke comes from a set of thick, muscular forearms. These, too, were developed in those early years.

"I built up my arms by swinging a barbell as a bat," Steve says. "And sometimes I'd use one of the Dodgers' broken bats. They were too heavy for me, but they made me strong in the arms for my age, from the elbows down, and that's the key to hitting."

Steve hit wherever he played, right into high school and American Legion ball. He was also a football star by then, a running back and defensive back who could pop through a hole or on defense pop a runner with gusto. He liked the gridiron almost as well as the diamond, and he excelled on both playing fields.

When he thinks back to his development as an athlete, Steve credits his coaches, and his own levelheaded philosophy, for his success.

"I've always been pleased with good coaches," he said, "all the way down the line through to the pros. Now I don't mean they were all the most knowledgeable coaches in the world, but they would still help me in some way to be a better baseball player, and I think that's a big reason for my success.

"Sometimes it was just the guidance I needed as a young player. I know I always listened as much as possible and tried to do the things I was instructed to do. Gradually, as I came to know myself better, I found out the things I was best suited for. All youngsters should try to do this. Anyway, after that, as I continued to grow, I tried to work on all the basic things, the basics of fielding, hitting the ball, and running the bases. Those basics can lay a good foundation for you to work on as you get older and begin to experiment with different things.

"I always tried to be an all-around ballplayer, both defensively and offensively, and a good thinking ballplayer as well. It pays off in the long run. Consistency is another thing that pays off. To be able to go out there each day and contribute something toward the success of the team is all anyone can ask of you."

By the time he reached high school he was a big star, one the scouts and recruiters were already watching closely. On the football field he had switched to quarterback, where his talents as a runner and a passer could be used best. In his senior year his gridiron record showed more than 1,000 yards gained running and more than 1,000 yards gained passing. It was quite a performance. Playing for his dream team, the Dodgers, was in the back of Steve's mind all along; but when he was offered a football scholarship to Michigan State University, he decided to take it.

Steve played both sports for the Spartans as a freshman, then in the autumn of his sophomore year he won a starting job as a defensive back on the varsity. That, in itself, is quite a tribute to Steve's ability, since Michigan State is in the Big Ten Conference, one of the best and most highly competitive in the country.

But Steve's Michigan State career didn't really last long. Shortly after the football season ended, the major leagues held its annual player draft, plucking youngsters from college campuses all around the country. Unlike football, the baseball draft does not have to wait until a youngster's class has graduated. And in 1968, Steve was drafted by none other than the Los Angeles Dodgers.

Steve promptly left Michigan State for the career that he'd always wanted, that of a professional baseball player—a Dodger. Of course, Garvey wasn't one to turn his back on education; he continued his studies in the off-season.

Being the top draft choice for the team of his choice was a big thrill, but Steve soon found he had to make some physical adjustments because of his preparation for football at Michigan State.

"A defensive back has a rough job," he said. "Most defensive backs aren't real big, but they've got to be strong because on running plays, for instance, I always had to take out the pulling guard and tackle. To build up for that, for taking out guys that weighed maybe 240 or 250, I had to work on the weights. So I had some pretty tight muscles and a football neck. When I gave up football for good and went into baseball, I quickly realized that I had to debulk, to stretch out all those muscles. It sounds easy, but when I look back I find that it took me about three years to get my body to the point that I wanted it, to stretch out all the right muscles and keep my strength in the right places. It's interesting, the way you have to control your body for the various sports."

To listen to Steve tell it, you'd think that he was a muscle-bound oaf his first couple of years in the Dodger organization. To him, maybe, but not to the casual observer or the record. The Dodgers sent him to Ogden, Utah, for the remainder of the 1968 season and in 62 games he batted .338, with 20 homers and 59 RBIs. It was apparent to everyone that they had a potentially fine hitter in the youngster from Tampa. Steve already had the quick bat and level swing, and he hung liners all over the field.

But Steve's field work was a different story. Steve was essentially a third baseman when he joined the Dodger organization, and he figured that was the place he'd play if and when he made it to the majors. But playing the hot corner was never easy for him. He knew immediately that he'd never be another Brooks Robinson. Throwing was a particular problem. He had separated a shoulder during freshman football at Michigan State, and while the injury wasn't a bad one, it seemed to have left him with something of a scatter arm. His throwing was erratic and unpredictable, and he'd often find himself flinging the ball over the first baseman's head or scaling it in the dirt well in front of the bag. His only consolation was that he was still in the low minors, probably a couple of years away from the parent club. He hoped that hard work and a lot of throwing would straighten it out.

The next year, 1969, Steve was at Albuquerque, New Mexico, where his strong bat once again did most of his talking. Despite a broken hand, which kept him out of the lineup for a couple of months, he still managed to hit .373 in 83 games. He had 14 homers and a very impressive total of 85 RBI's, a ratio that couldn't be ignored. The Dodgers even gave the youngster a brief taste of the majors that year, bringing him up at the tail end of the season for three games. Steve had a single in three trips to the plate and the thrill of major league action for the first time. But his fielding, if nothing else, dictated a bit more seasoning in the minors.

This time it was at Spokane of the Pacific Coast League, the Dodgers top farm club, and Steve responded with a .319 average in 95 games, once again proving himself a big run producer with 15 homers and 87 RBI's. His hitting earned him a longer stint with the Dodgers. He was in 34 games with L.A. that year, being used as a pinch hitter and part-time third baseman. He came to bat 95 times, with 25 hits and a .269 average. Not bad, though his power fell off noticeably. He produced just a single home run (his first in the majors) and drove in but six runs, a sorry total, especially for the intense Garvey, who knew that hitting would have to be his ticket to a major league job.

"The fielding was coming very slowly. My arm

was still wild. I couldn't always control my throws, and I was beginning to wonder whether I ever would on a regular basis. I've always been a bug on consistency and suddenly, in the field, it was the one thing I lacked. I knew I didn't have to be spectacular, but consistency was a must. So I dug in and worked harder."

In one sense, Steve came into the Dodger organization at the right time. Since the early 1940s, the Dodgers had usually been around the top of the league. There were pennants in 1941, 1947, 1949, 1952, 1953; a world championship in 1955 (their first); pennants in 1956 and 1959 (their first in Los Angeles); world championships in 1963 and 1965, and a pennant in 1966. That's 11 pennants and 3 world series wins in a 25-year span, a hard total to top.

Of course, during some of the interim years, there had to be rebuilding programs. The teams of the late forties and the fifties featured the so-called "Boys of Summer," the Dodgers that Steve first met in Tampa, the Hodges-Snider-Reese-Campanella-Furillo-Newcombe-Robinson-Gilliam teams that were as good as any. Then, in the 1960s, the club featured the likes of Sandy Koufax and Don Drysdale on the mound, Maury Wills, Tommy and Willie Davis, John Roseboro, and it got by on pitching and speed. Koufax retired with a bad elbow after the 1966 season, while some of the others began to fade. So it was time to rebuild again.

The Dodger skipper through both of the preceding eras was Walter Alston, who joined the team in 1954. He is still managing today, making him the dean of all major league pilots. Alston remembers the old Dodger teams well.

"The club when I joined it in 1954 was pretty much of a powerhouse," he recalls. "We had half a dozen guys who could reach the fence with no trouble. Playing in Ebbets Field (the team's ancient and smallish ball park in Brooklyn) helped, too. Add some good pitchers, and it was definitely a great ball club.

"In the sixties we had great pitching with Sandy and Don, pretty good defense, and concentrated speed in Wills and Willie Davis. So that club relied on its pitching, the stolen base, hit and run, squeeze plays, and stuff like that. We were in a big ball park in L.A. and were mainly a singles hitting team. We had to do it that way, but it worked."

Times had also changed as far as rebuilding a team was concerned, and Manager Alston talked about these differences, as well:

"In 1954, the Dodgers had a veteran team that was soon to begin fading. But the farm system was excellent in those days, very strong, and it didn't take too long to replace a Campanella with a Roseboro, a Reese with a Wills.

"But by the time that club began to fade in the late sixties, the farm system had changed. Now we had the draft and couldn't sign ballplayers at random, so it took a bit longer to rebuild. The Dodgers have always tried to develop their own players rather than trade for them, and we had to watch the farms very closely."

That's where Steve Garvey came in. He was among a group of youngsters coming onto the horizen from 1969 to 1971. Steve's first full year with the Dodgers was 1971, and it turned into one of the most frustrating of his career. He was a part-time player, and for the first time ever, he didn't really hit well; his average floundered around the .225 mark all season long.

Oddly enough, Steve had been the Dodgers opening-day third baseman in both 1970 and 1971. In 1970, he was soon returned to the minors, and in 1971 he was sent to the bench. His fielding was as erratic as ever, and when his hitting fell off, then there wasn't really much left.

Dodger fans were also getting anxious. Since that last pennant in 1966, the team had fallen to eighth and then seventh before the start of divisional play in 1969. They were fourth in the Western Division that year, then second in 1970. They seemed to be on the rise and the fans wanted a winner. That's one reason the boos came hard and fast when Steve Garvey's erratic arm went to work at third.

The second half of the 1971 season was a disaster for Steve. The team had improved and was headed toward a winning record, though no championship. But Steve was on the bench. Except for an occasional pinch-hitting assignment or spot start, he rarely played. He was nervous about another demotion to the minors, or worse yet, the possibility that his beloved Dodgers would trade him. After all, he hadn't really done anything to prove he could be a consistent, positive addition to the ball club. Steve recalls that bad time and a phone call that helped keep his courage up.

"The last half of the 1971 season I was in a very insecure position," he said. "Then, one night, I received a long distance call and heard my father's voice from Florida on the other end of the line. He said, 'I know this is the lowest point in your career. But remember, we love you and we're behind you one hundred percent. You're the model son.' When you hear words like that, you ask yourself, 'Can I be that bad off?' "

So Steve hung in there, though 1971 was not the kind of season to look back on with too much fondness. In 81 games Steve hit just .227, the lowest average of his professional life. He had just 7 homers and 26 RBI's, and he made a host of errors in the field. He knew he'd never be a regular with that kind of production.

Shortly after the season ended, Steve married his college sweetheart. Then Steve and Cyndy Garvey left for the Caribbean, not for a honeymoon, but so that Steve could play winter ball and try to improve his fielding.

He wasn't in the starting lineup when 1972 began, and Steve now feared his chance might never come, at least not with the Dodgers. He assumed they were thinking of him strictly as a utility player. Bill Grabarkewitz, who had finished 1971 strongly by subbing for Wills at shortstop, was given third base. He was considered a solid fielder and had hit well enough at the end of 1971 to merit a chance.

So Steve sat on the bench again and waited. This time around Grabarkewitz didn't hit a lick, and Garvey began getting into the lineup. But he never stayed long; his fielding and throwing still kept him from a regular job. As soon as he'd uncork a wild one, the fans would jump down his throat. Even his improved hitting didn't make much of a difference.

Steve was also learning just how nasty sports "fans" could be. He was booed unmercilessly. He also began receiving mail that was not only highly critical of his play but malicious and profane enough to be called "hate mail." He and Cyndy also began receiving phone calls that further berated him.

"I had to keep telling myself they were mad at the Dodger third baseman, not at Steve Garvey personally," he said. "Eventually you just have to tell them you can't talk to someone so irrational and then you have to hang up!"

Steve got into 96 games in 1972, as the Dodgers finished third in the Western Division with an 85-70 mark. His batting average was up from the year before at .269, but he had just 9 homers and 30 RBI's in 297 at bats. And he wasn't left in the lineup long enough to put anything together. How long could this kind of thing continue? So it was more winter ball and another effort to make himself into an adequate third sacker. Yet when the 1973 season began, Steve was once again on the bench, this time with a reacquired veteran, Ken McMullen at third.

The Dodger rebuilding program had also shifted gears. Several of the players who had come up around the same time as Garvey were no longer being counted on to bring the Dodgers back to the top. Youngsters like Ted Sizemore, Bill Sudakis, Bobby Valentine, Bill Grabarkewitz, and Jim Lefebvre were either traded or sitting on the bench. Some, such as Bill Russell and Davey Lopes, were changing position (they came from the outfield to take over at short and second). And another youngster, Ron Cey, was being groomed for a shot at third. Bill Buckner was playing first, but he could also play the outfield; while two new catchers, Joe Ferguson and Steve Yaeger, were also on hand. And Steve Garvey began to wonder if he, too, was being phased out.

It became more acute when McMullen bowed out at third and was immediately replaced by Cey. Alston had as much as said that the job was Cey's as long as he could keep it, and Cey was keeping it on an everyday basis.

The first two months of the 1973 season became a new low-point in Steve Garvey's career. He had started in less than a dozen games that year and was batting .228.

"It was the definite low-point," he recalls. "With each passing day it began to look more and more as if Cey was the third baseman. He wasn't about to be moved out. I was hardly playing at all, just pinch hitting occasionally and sometimes not getting in for two weeks because I didn't have a position. I was really starting to get down. But finally I just said to myself, if I'm ever going to get anywhere with this team, I've just got to do it when the opportunity comes—any opportunity."

So Steve dug in, and the next time Manager Alston called on him to pinch hit, he went up to the plate with more concentration and determination than ever before. Pinch hitting isn't easy. A player comes up cold: he hasn't been in the game and the muscles aren't limber. Not everyone can do it. Even some of the game's best hitters have been repeatedly frustrated when called upon to be pinch swingers. When Steve went up there he just tried to isolate his concentration on the pitcher, as he would if he were a regular. He promptly smashed a solid single to left.

From that point on, Steve became a pinch hitter extraordinaire. He banged out 10 hits in 24 pinch-hitting situations, and that's a .417 clip. His hits weren't cheapies either; they were solid line drives, many coming in clutch spots with the game on the line. Even a good number of his outs were on solid shots. He was making contact with consistency, and people in the Dodger camp were taking notice.

The problem was what to do with him. Ron Cey was asserting himself at third. He was showing fine potential at the plate and a consistency in the field. So to reinsert Garvey at third was out. In fact, there were young players at almost every position. Yet some kind of decision had to be made. By all the evidence, including his latest pinch-hitting spree, Steve Garvey had what it takes to be a fine major league batter. Finally, Alston came up with a solution.

In 1970 and 1971, another young ballplayer named Bill Buckner has been an outfield starter. Then, in 1972, with the retirement of all-star first baseman, Wes Parker, Buckner had come in and played first. This was because the Dodgers had acquired outfielder Frank Robinson in a trade. Buckner was again at first when 1973 began, but Robinson had been traded away and there was an outfield spot open if Alston wanted to move him. Without warning, Alston told Buckner he'd be returning to left, where he was outstanding, and he handed a first-baseman's mitt to Steve Garvey.

"I want you in there every day," he told Garvey. "And we feel you'll be able to do the job at first."

At first Steve was dumbfounded. He had played some first base during his career, but not in the majors, and he never really considered himself a first baseman. But with characteristic determination, he took the glove and immediately began learning about the new position (the same position played by his early idol, Gil Hodges).

Some people consider first an easy position, a dumping ground for players who can't cut it anywhere else. For years, first base has been a kind of preservation ground for aging outfielders, so they can save their legs for hitting. Mickey Mantle, Willie Mays, and Henry Aaron all played some first base in the latter stages of their careers, but none of them found it an easy task!

It's one thing to play first base, and it's another to play it well. It's more than just catching the ball. Neither Mantle, Mays, nor Aaron, for instance, was ever really comfortable at first. Aaron, for one, asked to return to the outfield. In fact, the only all-star outfielder who has become an all-star-caliber first baseman late in his career has been the Red Sox Carl Yastrzemski. And Yaz is just a fielding natural.

There had to be question marks both in Steve Garvey's mind and in the minds of the Dodger brass when the stocky youngster went out to first base with no practical experience. For one thing, managers like first baseman to be tall and rangy, so they can go up for those high throws and stretch out for the close ones. When you think of a typical first baseman a player like Willie "Stretch" McCovey comes to mind. His lanky, 6'-

4″ frame has turned many potential wild throws and close plays into outs. Many thought that Garvey, at 5′-10″, was too short to play the position effectively.

Garvey had plenty of help from Buckner and the Dodger coaches, and he concentrated on learning the footwork and other skills needed around the bag. Fortunately, he didn't let it affect his hitting. He immediately went on a tear that saw him hit safely in nine of his first ten games. And the hits came in bunches, two or three to a game, raising his batting average up over the .300 mark in a matter of weeks. And to the surprise of everyone, he was doing a nice job at first. The experiment was working.

To the surprise of many, Steve was making one of the most difficult aspects of playing first—digging low throws out of the dirt—look easy. Some players can never do it well, but Steve was scooping them out as if he had been doing it all his life. He was also showing a remarkable ability to recover and make sweep tags on plays that saw him pulled off the bag, and this compensated somewhat for his lack of height and reach. Because of this, he had perhaps more collisions at first than most first sackers, but this didn't bother him at all. After all, as an ex-football player, he was used to contact. Dodger Coach Monty Basgall, who was helping and observing Steve constantly during this period of transition, often marveled at the tenacity with which Steve went after charging base runners.

"He's not afraid of any physical thing in the world," the coach said.

As for Steve, he was overjoyed with everything.

He was finally getting the chance to play, was hitting very well, and gathering additional confidence with each passing game. For the first time since coming up to the Dodgers, he felt he would remain in the lineup, that he had finally found a place for himself.

"I think first base is more my natural position," Steve told reporters. "In the past most of my errors have been throwing errors and not fielding errors, and I really haven't had any major problems adjusting. The nice thing is that Manager Alston agrees about it, too."

With Steve's run-producing bat in the lineup every day, the Dodgers resumed their chase of the front-running Cincinnati Reds in the National League's Western Division. It was a young Dodger team on the field now, and many observers felt they had a good chance to catch the Reds in 1973, and if not, they would definitely be a factor in the ensuing seasons. Ferguson and Yaeger continued to split the catching duties; Garvey was at first; the speedy, base-stealing Davey Lopes was at second; the improving Bill Russell was at short; and steady Ron Cey was at third. The outfield now consisted of Buckner in left; veteran Willie Davis in center; and another youngster, Willie Crawford, in right. Alston also had some veteran reserves with whom he could platoon or replace if necessary.

Only the pitching was suspect. Newly acquired Andy Messersmith, veteran Don Sutton, and veteran Tommy John were the principal starters. Another reliable starter or two was needed. The bullpen was dependable, if not spectacular, but as Alston himself had said:

"Our team in the late fifties was pretty much of a powerhouse, while our title teams of the sixties did it with speed and pitching. This club is probably the best balanced of all."

It was Steve Garvey, to a large degree, who provided the final cog in the wheel of balance. For the remainder of the 1973 season Garvey gave the club something he had striven for since coming up. He was consistent not only at the plate but also in the field. He kept his average above the .300 mark for the entire second half of the season, hitting consistently and driving in runs. He was playing every day for the first time in his career and was improving at first with each passing game. In fact, he was becoming an outstanding first baseman, something which even the most optimistic of Dodgers had not expected.

The Dodgers played very well during the second half of 1973, but Cincy kept up its hot pace. Although Los Angeles finished with a 95-66 record, their best since 1965, they finished second in their division to the Reds. Yet the future augured very well for L.A.

The future also looked bright for Garvey. He completed his best and most satisfying season ever by hitting .304, the best on the team among the players participating in more than 100 games. He had wound up playing in 114, banging out 106 hits in 349 at bats, including 8 homers and 50 RBI's. He had also 17 doubles and 3 triples.

When the season was over, someone asked Garvey about his sudden success. Of course, a great deal of it was triggered by the fact that he played every day, but the articulate Garvey saw it as something more as well.

"I guess the difference would be intensity and concentration," he said. "I've learned to block out everything else when I get out onto the field. It's so important to be able to concentrate. You just can't succeed when your mind is wandering.

"It's rough enough to hit a baseball, you know, a round ball and a round bat, and you've got to hit it square. You just can't do it consistently unless your concentration is complete. The same goes in the field. You've got to be concentrating on every situation, so you know exactly what to do without hesitation. Otherwise, you'll lose that important split second, or you'll blow the play completely.

"So I think the difference between a really successful athlete and an athlete who has the same ability but who only performs to the average level is dedication, intensity, and concentration."

When Steve came to the Dodger camp in Florida to begin the 1974 season, he came with a new feeling of security. He had a job, and what's more, the Dodgers seemed ready to make a real run for the National League pennant. The club had made two key trades which they hoped would put them over the top. They first brought center fielder Jim Wynn from Houston. Wynn, a diminutive slugger, had had some personal problems while playing for the Astros. The Dodgers figured he would add power to their attack. Then they took their previous centerfielder, Willie Davis, and traded him to Montreal for relief pitcher Mike Marshall. Marshall was an effective fireman with one exceptional quality. He had a tireless arm and could pitch nearly every day if called upon. In fact, he had set a major league record by appearing in 92 games for the Expos in 1973 and had indicated he wanted to work even more in 1974.

The Dodgers started the season with a bang, winning early and winning big. It seemed as if everyone was hitting. Wynn was particularly conspicuous in his new surroundings, as he jumped atop the league in homers and RBI's. There were also major contributions from Buckner, Russell, Lopes, and Cey, as well as Garvey, who was stinging the ball as well as he had at the end of 1973. He wasn't getting much notice, however, because of Wynn's flashy start.

By the end of May the Dodgers were really rolling. They already had a seven-game lead over Cincinnati and were pacing both leagues in almost every major batting and pitching category.

Wynn, known as the "Toy Cannon," led the league in homers with 12 and in RBI's with 37. His batting average was up around the .330 mark. Left fielder Buckner was carrying on at about .340, while Willie Crawford, Russell, and Cey were all in the .290's. As for Steve, he had silently crept up to number two in homers with 8 and was hitting around .320. Before the year was out, his consistency would overshadow all the rest.

The club was also getting good pitching, especially from starters Messersmith and Sutton and from reliever Marshall, who was proving to be all that was said about him. He was pitching well and at a pace that seemed to target him for a 100-game season. It was hard to conceive of anyone pitching that often, but then again, everything was going right for the Dodgers. That sentiment was quickly echoed by Manager Alston.

"Sure, I'll admit things have gone just right for us," he said. "We've won a few that maybe we shouldn't have, but we've also been working hard to stay one step ahead of our opponents. This is a very sound ball club. Just look at it this way. We won ninety-five games last year with a bunch of inexperienced kids, and that year of experience is really paying off this time around."

Experience plus newcomers Wynn and Marshall and the full-time services of Steve Garvey were the ingredients that made the difference. Garvey was quickly proving that the second half of the 1973 season was no fluke.

He was becoming the steadying influence on the team, as his consistency went unmatched throughout the year. His average was above .300 all season long, and he never went more than three games without getting a hit. His line drives were producing runs at an impressive clip, and his fielding at first was better than ever.

As midseason approached, the Dodgers were still first by a comfortable margin. Now the All-Star Game was coming up and the fans began filing their votes for the starters. The latest method for electing the starting team was for the fans to obtain a printed ballot from the league. The ballot was broken down by positions, and under each position were the names of the players most likely to be candidates, in other words, the five or six men considered the best at their respective positions. Because he was still a virtual unknown when the ballots were printed, Garvey's name wasn't on it.

There is a provision for write-in votes on the ballot, but the fans usually find it easier to put a check next to a name rather than write one in. That makes it doubly difficult for a player to make the team via the write-in route. So Steve's expectations weren't too high.

Fortunately, baseball fans can be a knowledgeable lot. There are surely times when they'll vote for a perennial favorite, a tried veteran, instead of a "hot" player. But in Steve's case they saw the light. The write-in votes began coming in in droves —by the hundreds, the thousands, the hundreds of thousands. When the final tally was in, Steve Garvey had made the National League All-Star team by virtue of more than a million write-in votes.

"This is obviously the thrill of a lifetime for me," Steve said. "I didn't think it was possible. It's another one of my boyhood dreams come true, and I never thought it would happen like this or so quickly. I hope I don't let the fans down."

He didn't. In the true Frank Merriwell tradition, Steve was not only in the game, he dominated it. Using that short, compact swing against unsuspecting American League pitchers, he crashed out two key hits and then made a diving stop in the field to choke off an A.L. threat. The National League had still another All-Star win, and Steve Garvey received a trophy as the game's Most Valuable Player. It was rapidly becoming a storybook season for him.

The second half of the year continued to show that Garvey was no fluke. In fact, during that second half, he began to emerge as the field leader of the Dodgers. A nagging injury slowed Wynn's pace; while Buckner, Cey, Lopes, and Russell all had their streaky spots. But Garvey was like the

Rock of Gibraltar. Day in and day out he was in the lineup and contributing. He was batting fourth now, the clean-up spot. While he wasn't the classic slugger, he was getting the job done, taking over from Wynn as the club RBI leader and staying up among the league's best. He was the man the Dodgers knew they could depend on to get the job done.

He was also becoming one of the most popular Dodgers in other ways. Remembering how he felt as a youngster when a player like Gil Hodges spoke with him and signed an autograph, Steve tried to relate to youngsters in the same way. He knew there were athletes who didn't give autographs, but he felt he had an obligation to the fans. He was representing not only himself, but the Dodger organization and baseball as a whole. So whenever possible he signed and gave a friendly, smiling word to youngsters and fans of all ages.

No one could blame Steve, of course, for being a happy man. He was putting the wraps on a great season and the Dodgers were putting the wraps on the Western Division title, taking it with relative ease after leading all the way. And when it ended, people began to realize just how great a season Steve Garvey had had.

The rough figures read this way: .312 batting average, 21 home runs, 111 runs batted in, 200 hits, 95 runs scored. In the field Steve Garvey made just eight errors all year, earning him the Gold Glove Award as the best fielder in the league at his position. Not bad for an error-prone infielder. But his hitting was the big thing, and most people figured it would be needed as the Dodgers went up against the Pittsburgh Pirates in a three of five series for the National League pennant.

If the Los Angeles team had any weaknesses, they were on the mound, where there were just two reliable starters in Messersmith (20 wins) and Sutton (19). But the club had Mike Marshall, who had set an unbelievable major league record by appearing in 106 of the Dodgers 162 games, pitching 208⅓ innings of relief (winning 15 and saving 21). He was soon to become the first relief pitcher ever to win the Cy Young Award. The Dodgers figured they'd need Marshall against the Pirates, which was one of the best hitting teams in baseball.

Yet the pitching was better than the Dodgers expected. Sutton, who had won 13 of his last 14 decisions in the regular season shut out the Pirates in the first game, 3-0. In the second game Messersmith and Marshall combined for a 5-2 Los Angeles win. Pittsburgh bounded back to take the third, but Sutton returned to the mound for the fourth game, which was played before nearly 55,000 fans in Los Angeles.

Steve had been relatively quiet in the first three games, coming through with a couple of singles, but not doing anything spectacular. But the fourth game was all his. Wynn doubled home a Dodger run in the first. Then in the third with two out, Wynn walked. Up came Steve, facing left-hander Jerry Reuss. Reuss tried to keep the ball away from the right-handed batting Garvey, but Garvey went with the pitch and sent a liner to right center. It wasn't a towering drive, but the power behind it carried it over the wall for a two-run homer. The Dodgers led 3-0.

Then in the fifth, Wynn walked again. This time left-hander Ken Brett was on the mound. He tried to curve Garvey, and this time the liner was pulled to left. Again it cleared the wall for another two-run homer. It gave the Dodgers a 5-0 lead and just about put the game on ice.

The Dodgers just rolled it up after that, winning the game and the pennant, 12-1, as Steve had two more hits and wound up with a .389 average for the four-game series. Now the Dodgers were World Series bound. They would meet the Oakland A's, a team that had won the world's championship the previous two seasons.

In the A's, the Dodgers would be facing a team that was in many ways similar, but in many ways their opposite. Both were California based, making for the first "freeway" series, but while the Dodgers were generally considered as one big happy family, the A's were involved in more battles than Napoleon.

Known as the Fighting A's, the club was constantly in turmoil. Players were ever at odds with flamboyant owner Charles O. Finley, and almost all of the team's stars were either taking pot shots at Finley in the press or asking to be traded. During the 1973 series, which the A's won from the New York Mets, the players threatened to boycott when Finley dismissed a utility player, Mike Andrews, because he had made two errors in a crucial game. And when they weren't fighting with Finley, they were battling among themselves. Right before the start of the 1974 classic, there was a clubhouse brawl between pitchers Blue Moon Odom and Rollie Fingers. It wasn't the first time those kinds of shenanigans had gone on.

But despite this the team was loaded with top talent, such as pitcher Catfish Hunter (who was suing Finley for breach of contract and eventually became a free agent), Vida Blue (who once held out for over a month to protest Finley's contract offer), and Ken Holtzman (who perennially threatened retirement as a protest over Finley's actions).

The other players were just as notable. Outfielder Reggie Jackson (the biggest Finley baiter of them all) was considered the team's top slugger and superstar. Outfielder Joe Rudi, third baseman Sal Bando, first sacker Gene Tenace, and shortstop Bert Campaneris were other top players who had contributed to Series victories over the Cincinnati Reds and New York Mets. The A's were no team to mess with, yet for some reason the Dodgers were solid favorites when the fall classic began.

Lefty Holtzman was facing Messersmith in game one, played in Los Angeles. The A's struck first when right fielder Jackson, hobbled by a pulled hamstring muscle, stroked one over the left field wall. Then in the fifth, pitcher Holtzman doubled, went to third on a wild pitch, and scored when Campaneris executed a perfect suicide squeeze bunt. The final Oakland run came in the eighth on a single, sacrifice, and wild throw by third baseman Cey. The Dodgers got one back in the fifth on a pair of Oakland errors and another on a Wynn homer in the ninth. Garvey followed Wynn's homer with a single, but then Catfish Hunter came out of the bullpen to strike out Joe Ferguson to end the game. Oakland had won it, 3-2.

Sutton pitched the Dodgers back into it with a 3-2 win of his own in game two. The first run came in off Vida Blue on a walk and two singles, the next two on a single by Garvey and homer by Ferguson. But that wasn't all Garvey contributed to the victory.

With one out in the Oakland eighth, pinch hitters Jim Holt and Claudell Washington smacked back-to-back singles. An error by Russell on a Campaneris grounder loaded the bases with speedy Bill North at bat.

North hit a sharp grounder up the middle. Shortstop Russell cut it off, stepped on second, and fired to first, hoping for a double play. The ball was low, bounding in the dirt several feet in front of the stretching Garvey. But Steve stayed cool, as he had all year. With a sweeping motion of his glove he scooped the ball up in time to nip North. The rally was over.

"It was the key play of the game," said the A's Sal Bando. "If he doesn't catch that ball, we have two runs and a man on second."

But Steve was used to low throws. "I'm not as tall as most first basemen," he said, "and I think my infielders are in fear of throwing over my head. So they're more conscious of keeping the ball down and consequently throw in the dirt quite often. I must have had thirty or thirty-five of those pickups this year, and I'm getting pretty much accustomed to it."

So the series was tied at one and still a tossup. But no one was prepared for what would happen in the next three games. In fact, one Dodger made the mistake of berating the A's before the third game. He said:

"We won 104 games during the season; they won 88. And they look to me like an 88-game club."

It wasn't the wisest thing in the world to say, especially when Oakland's postseason play had been so good the past two years. As is usually the case, someone pinned a copy of the remarks in the Oakland clubhouse, and they used it to fire themselves up before the remaining games.

For the remainder of the series the A's played brilliantly in the field, while the Dodgers began looking more and more like a bunch of inexperienced youngsters. It was Al Downing against Catfish Hunter in game three. The A's got two in the third when catcher Joe Ferguson made a pair of errors and one more in the fourth. The Dodgers got single tallies in the eighth and ninth on homers by Buckner and Crawford, but the game ended at 3-2.

Game four was pivotal, and in a special sense, a game Steve Garvey would never forget. It wasn't his hitting he'd remember, though he was the only Dodger making good contact on a regular basis. In fact, it wasn't even the result of the game that would stick in his memory. In the early innings, Garvey learned that his wife had given birth to a daughter, Krisha Lee Garvey. He said he was "trying to hit one for Krisha" that day, but he had to settle for a couple of solid singles. Unfortunately, there was little help from his Dodger mates.

The A's went ahead 1-0 on a homer by pitcher Holtzman. Then the Dodgers took a 2-1 lead when Garvey singled, Ferguson walked, and Russell cracked a triple between a drawn-in outfield.

But Andy Messersmith couldn't hold the lead. In the sixth the A's rallied, scored four times, and held on for a 5-2 victory. They now led three games to one, and the Dodgers seemed all but finished.

Neither team was really powdering the ball, but the A's (especially their second baseman, Dick Green) were fielding beautifully. Green made several miraculous stops which he turned into double plays ending Dodger rallies. So not even the breaks were working for L.A.

It was Sutton versus Blue in game five—the A's trying to wrap it up, the Dodgers trying to stave off defeat. In the first inning the A's Bill North tried to steal second and catcher Yaeger promptly threw the ball into centerfield. A sacrifice fly by Sal Bando made it 1-0. Then in the second, A's catcher Ray Fosse homered to make it 2-0. Dodger hopes were fading.

L.A. still had one gasp left. They got runners on second and third in the sixth. Wynn brought one home with a sacrifice fly, and then Steve drove in the tying tally with a sharp single before the A's closed out the threat. In the bottom of the seventh the Dodgers had relief ace Marshall on the mound. The game was halted temporarily as fans in the left field stands began throwing debris at left fielder Buckner. When the game resumed Joe Rudi was up. He saw that Marshall hadn't taken any warmup tosses during the delay, so he dug in for the first pitch. Sure enough, it didn't have anything on it, and Rudi belted it into the seats for a go-ahead homer.

The Dodgers had a chance to tie in the eighth when Buckner opened with a single. When the ball skipped past center fielder North, Buckner raced to second. Only he didn't stop, he gambled and headed to third. Once again the A's came through. Two perfect throws cut down the sliding Buckner and the rally was nipped right then and there. Rollie Fingers, who was to become series MVP, retired the Dodgers in the eighth and ninth to nail down the victory. The A's had won in five games.

It was a bitter disappointment for the young Dodger team. They hadn't played well. In fact, neither team had hit much: the A's had .211; the Dodgers had .228. The leading hitter among the regulars on both teams was Steve Garvey. Steady as usual, Garvey had 8 hits in 21 at bats for a .381 average. No other Dodger regular hit above .250. One writer, in fact, called Garvey "the noblest Dodger of them all."

The gloom of losing was lifted somewhat for Steve Garvey several weeks after the season ended. That's when he learned he had been chosen the Most Valuable Player in the National League. It was quite an honor, but it didn't come without controversy. Many people thought the prize should have gone to the great St. Louis Card veteran Lou Brock, who, at age thirty-five, had set an amazing record by stealing 118 bases during the season. Naturally, many writers asked Steve about his selection and about the way the award was given.

"As with most awards now," Steve said, "there are three or four guys who have an excellent chance, and it just depends on how the voters see it. Lou Brock is a man of integrity. I admire him. He's a great ballplayer, and I know he was let down. Anyone would be. But I think the award was voted on justly.

"Some people feel the players should pick the MVP, not the writers, since they perform alongside and opposite each other all year. But the writers are on the scene for the entire season as well. So I guess you could make an argument for each side. It's just six of one, half a dozen of the other."

The MVP prize certainly had an effect on Steve's life. There were requests for many more public appearances, some off-field endorsements (such as a public relations job for a major soft drink company), and coupled with his great season, ammunition to practically double his salary into the $90,000 range.

Steve welcomed the public appearances because he felt they gave him a chance to talk about "some of the things I believe in." That's when he got his reputation as the all-American boy. He was always clean-cut, impeccably dressed, hair short and in place. He talked only about good, positive things—the virtues of sport, of God, of America—and about the "death of the anti-hero." It allowed him to be a "twelve month a year baseball promoter." But it was these very things that began to annoy some of his teammates during the 1975 season.

It was a season of bitter disappointment for the Dodgers. To begin with, the Cincinnati Reds got off to a fast start and never slowed down, putting the Dodgers in the back seat at the start. And playing catch-up isn't very easy, as the Reds had found out the year before. Then there were the injuries. It seemed as if they came in bunches.

The team suffered nearly fifty injuries in 1975. At various times the following key players were on the shelf for extended periods: Sutton, Wynn, Marshall, Ferguson, Russell, and Buckner. Though the team finished with an 88-74 mark, they were some twenty games behind Cincinnati, which burned all year and wound up 108-54. The Dodgers were never in it, and when a team is going badly, the resentments begin to surface.

Steve saw it coming, since he was having another super season.

"There were feelings and vibrations and little remarks," he told a writer. "I just put them out of my mind because I didn't want somebody's little remark to interfere with my job. But when it came out publicly there was no more disillusioned person with professional sports than myself, because I couldn't believe anyone would say anything publicly against a teammate. It was the ultimate slap in the face. I could have handled it one-on-one if they'd come to me directly."

The remarks allegedly had to do with Steve's goodie-goodie image and his promotional zeal for his own lifestyle. One story appeared in a San Bernardino paper which claimed that several anonymous teammates resented the way Steve had been acting. There was even criticism of Steve's wife, Cyndy, for "sticking her face in front of the cameras." And one player came right out and said:

"I don't mind what Steve does. If he wants to

go out of his way to be a clean-cut kid, that's fine, as long as he doesn't interfere with my style. Sometimes, he has interfered."

There were allegedly apologies at a team meeting, but some say things were never the same that year with the Dodgers.

"Steve told me he was glad in a way that it happened," Cyndy Garvey told a reporter. "It showed him how he stood with the team. In some ways it made him more secure in the way he is. He does the things he does because he is that way. He believes what he says, and he won't change to please someone else."

Steve tried to analyze and explain the problem, or what he felt it to be.

"I think there is more jealousy in a team sport than an individual sport," he said. "As a rule you have one or two people behind you for a position, and there is a competitiveness to be the best. You have a group of guys who came up with a common goal, to reach the highest level they possibly can. When they make the majors they've made it, and the next thing is to lead the team. In baseball you see what every individual does. There has to be a little jealousy or vanity for somebody who may be doing a little better.

"I think jealousy had something to do with it in this case. I don't *do* anything. I've never tried to convert anyone. Maybe sometimes my doing things, like signing autographs or making appearances, puts pressure on other guys to do the same thing. But that's not it. If you feel like doing these things, you do them. Maybe they thought I was setting an example. . . . If we got attention it was not because we asked for it. People came to us for interviews."

On the field, Steve was one of the few Dodgers to have an outstanding season. He upped his batting average to .319, tied Pete Rose for second place in the hit parade with 210 (behind Dave Cash's 213), whacked out 18 homers and drove home 95 more runs. He had another banner year in the field with just 8 errors. He was truly an all-star again and one of the young superstars of the game.

Perhaps there was some jealousy involved, perhaps Steve is sometimes overzealous in talking about baseball, God, and country. Regardless of the reasons, no one can accuse either Steve or Cyndy Garvey of being anything but completely honest. They have both talked about the false glamour in an athlete's life, how it's difficult to run a household and raise a family, of the loneliness a wife experiences when her husband is away, of how it's sometimes difficult to find privacy or have time alone, of how a baseball wife has to sacrifice and change her life because it's virtually impossible for the husband to change his schedule. And in this way the Garveys are refreshing to have around.

And the way Steve Garvey plays ball, he's obviously going to be around for some time to come. It's fairly safe to assume that when and if the Dodgers start winning again (they certainly have youth and talent on their side), the petty differences will be forgotten. For on the field every team needs a leader, a man they can look to for the big hit, the big play, an inspirational lift. And in two outstanding seasons since becoming a regular, Steve Garvey has shown he can do the job. He has some awful large shoes from the team's past to fill, but as Steve himself has often said:

"I was born to be a Dodger."

Lou Brock

It was still early in the 1973 baseball season, but Lou Brock was worried. The fleet left fielder of the St. Louis Cardinals didn't feel he was running well. He was rapidly approaching his thirty-fourth birthday, and suddenly the stolen bases weren't coming.

Stolen bases had been a major part of Lou Brock's game for some time. In fact, he had set a major league record by stealing fifty or more bases for eight consecutive seasons, beginning in 1965. So he was already regarded as one of the master base thiefs of all time—as well as an outstanding all-around player, a "money player," a clutch performer who knew how to win. Yet despite all this, Brock was worried.

"I had been thrown out thirteen of the first twenty-three times I ran," he recalls, "and I was getting all kinds of negative vibes running through my head. I was almost thirty-four years old, and I figured I had slowed up. I thought I couldn't run anymore. I remember one day I was stealing and I just stopped. Stopped cold in the middle of the baseline. I thought I heard the bat-

ter hit a foul ball, but he hadn't even swung, and
I was a sitting duck."

The incident put another dent in Brock's rapidly ebbing confidence. After eight seasons as a
superthief, the best base runner in the majors,
Lou felt it all slipping away. And he had always
maintained that once the skills began to go, he'd
quit rather than hang on like so many other players. For the first time since he broke in with the
Cubs back in 1962, Lou Brock thought the end
was in sight.

Then Brock ran into Maury Wills. Wills was the
superthief of the preceding generation, having set
a record in 1962 with 104 swipes. Wills was a
sportscaster in 1973, an astute observer of the
game, and as soon as he saw Lou he knew what
was troubling him.

"Maury didn't mince words," said Lou. "He
told me right away to just keep running and not
to count the times I was caught. That was the big
thing. I took his advice, and pretty soon it all
started coming together again."

It came together, all right. Brock finished the
1973 season with 70 steals, good enough to lead
the league once again, and the second best total
of his career. He obviously hadn't slowed up. In
fact, by season's end, people were saying he was
better than ever.

Yet no one suspected what was to come in
1974. If anything, most baseball people felt
Brock would slow down somewhat. After all, he'd
be nearly thirty-five years old, and at that age it
isn't easy stealing 60 or 70 bases. Most reasoned
that the wear and tear would be too great. Brock's
skills might enable him to get another 50 or so,

but he was too smart a player to push it too hard. He wouldn't put his body on the line for another 10 or 15 steals. He'd pace himself more than even before. Veteran ballplayers usually do that at age thirty-five. They just can't go every day like they used to ten years earlier.

But Brock fooled them all. Taking up where he left off in 1973, he ran, and ran, and ran. By mid-season he already had his 50 steals, and people were beginning to talk about a new record. They were also wondering if Brock's body could take the beating.

He showed them, not by slowing down or pacing himself, but by running even more. In a weekend series against the Phillies in early August, the 5'-11", 170-pounder not only banged out 10 hits in 17 at bats but also swiped 8 bases in 9 attempts. Talk of a new record increased, and so did Brock's pace. By the time he got his hundredth and hundred and first steals (against the Mets on September 6), it was obvious that only an injury could prevent Brock from breaking the mark.

Steal number 104, against the Phils, not only tied the record but also gave Brock a National League career mark of 739 steals. By the time the season ended, the baseball world stood in awe of the thirty-five-year-old superstar. At an age when most players were looking toward retirement, Lou Brock had set an amazing record. In 153 games, he had stolen 118 bases!

It was a truly momentous feat, made even greater by considering Brock's age and the cases of baseball's other premier base stealers, Maury Wills and the immortal Ty Cobb.

Wills was approaching thirty when he swiped his 104 in 1962, while Cobb was not yet twenty-nine the year he pilfered 96, way back in 1915. And both men testified to the bumps and bruises, the toll that stealing so many bases took on their bodies. They were constantly nursing scrapes and sores; running on fragile, tired legs; finishing the season nearly exhausted.

Yet Brock, some six years or so older than the other two, finished as fast or faster than he started, missing just nine games, and six of those were the result of a shoulder injury suffered in the outfield. The steals seem to come easy.

The answer lies in his approach to base running. Brock's approach is distinctly different from both Cobb's and Wills'. Ty Cobb was the best ballplayer of his generation, and in the minds of many, the best of all time. He was a fiery soul, an intense competitor who would do anything to win a ball game. He made himself a base stealer and studied every possible way of getting an advantage once he reached base. And he reached base more than anyone else, getting more than 4,000 hits during his long career.

As a base runner he was a terror. He had better than average speed, which he used to the maximum, but he also let it be known that his spikes would come in high if the situation called for it. Not that Cobb was a dirty player. He once said he only spiked two players intentionally during his playing days. But he also said that baseball was "an unrelenting war of nerves," and he used that psychology to instill a kind of fear in opposing players. Fear of Cobb's spikes did as much damage as the spikes themselves.

But base running was still a bruising business for Cobb. There were plenty of head-on collisions, and to avoid them, Cobb used a variety of slides and maneuvers.

"The whole secret of sliding is to make your move at the last possible second," Cobb once said. "When I went in there I wanted to see the whites of the fielder's eyes. I liked to come straight at him, then collapse right or left after perhaps faking the other way.

"Sometimes I'd deliberately slide wide, go past the bag, then reach back and hook the outside corner with my trailing toe. And there were times when I'd go even further past and reach back with my hand to get the bag."

Combining all this with the rough, unkempt infields of the day, many of which were loaded with pebbles and small stones, and Cobb was one beat-up ballplayer by the time August and September rolled around. Guts and courage kept him going, but his body took a terrific beating.

There were many other top base runners in Cobb's day. That's the way the game was played. But when Maury Wills came up in 1959, the home run had already taken over the running game. The base stealing title in the 1950s was often won with under 30 steals. Yet that didn't deter Wills. He went about the business of learning to run the bases against National League pitchers. In his second season, 1960, he took his first base-stealing crown, with 50 thefts. Two years later he would set a new standard with 104. So with Wills leading the way, base running began to reappear, and once again many young players began running.

Wills was no one-shot wonder. He reached the majors later than most, but he had a second big year in 1965, with 94 steals, when he was already thirty-three. Wills was a lot like Ty Cobb in that he played the game at a high intensity and pulled out all stops to steal a base or help in a victory. At 5'–10", 165-pounds, his body took a pounding from his slides and competitive tactics. In fact, after his record-breaking 1962 season, he fell off in 40 steals in 1963; and after his 94 steals in 1965, he dropped to 38. It might have been the pounding.

Lou Brock has avoided that kind of thing. He is perhaps the most consistent base stealer of all time, as his record of 11 consecutive 50-steal seasons attests. He has perhaps the most clinical approach to stealing of all the great ones. He does it the same way every time. He uses the same slide, which happens to be the safest and least damaging, and in that way avoids some of the bruising pitfalls that made stealing a painful proposition to the others.

"I saw Maury Wills run quite often," Brock says. "He used the hook slide almost exclusively. That means he's always going for the corner of the base. It's a beautiful but damaging slide, because a larger portion of your body—legs, rump, arms, elbows, and even back—can make contact with the ground. I always use the straight-in, or 'pop-up', slide. That way, just my calves absorb any real contact or punishment."

It all sounds pretty simple: Brock gets to first, Brock takes off, Brock slides straight into second, Brock has another stolen base. Very neat and clean. But although Brock's technique is clinical, it's a technique that has been developed, step by step, for many years.

"It's been years of practice and torture for me," Brock said during his record-breaking season. "First of all, it's learning to read the pitchers. Every base runner must do this if he expects to steal successfully. By reading the pitcher he knows when to run and when he can get his best jump.

"This is directly related to leading. The amount of lead a runner takes is related to confidence and his ability to read the pitcher. He's got to know he can get back and must know just how far he can go before he's in no-man's land, the point of no return. So it's essential to establish an association with first base. You can't watch the pitcher and keep looking back to the base. You never beat a pitcher by guessing where you are. This is a precise business, with no place for error.

"The initial thrust is another absolute must. A runner can practice and improve upon this. He's got to be able to move out and be at maximum speed within ten steps or so. It's a matter of power and thrust and can be achieved through hard work."

These are still all basics, basics that not every fast runner can achieve, but basics nevertheless. After that, it's a matter of further refinement. That is where the real science comes in, where the men are separated from the boys. And this is where Lou Brock is a total artist.

"I have a decided advantage over the pitcher," Lou says, "because I can change my stealing technique, but a pitcher's motion is mechanical. He cannot alter it without risking injury to his arm.

By using varying lengths and styles of leads and takeoffs, I minimize detection of my plans.

"All pitchers fall into four broad catagories. The anatomy of their bodies dictates what moves they have to make. I rate moves as fast, quick, moderate, and slow. Believe it or not, a pitcher can be slow and quick. So you've got to learn it all.

"Another factor is the stuff the pitcher has. If you have a sinker ball pitcher, the catcher will have to come up more before he gets the ball off. But when there's a fastballer, say like Tom Seaver, on the mound, the ball just zings in there, and the catcher is ready to get the peg off a split-second sooner. And that can be the difference."

Both Brock and Maury Wills acknowledge that it was more difficult stealing more than 100 bases in 1974 than it was in 1962. Says Wills:

"In some ways the record was more difficult for Lou than it was for me. At the time I broke Cobb's mark everyone was home run conscious, and the pitchers weren't used to keeping runners close to first. I could get some pretty good leads.

"But after I stole 104 the game kind of changed. Pitchers started working on keeping the good base runners close to first and not letting them get a huge jump."

Brock looks at it in terms of the catchers. "When I first came up there wasn't that much stealing and the catchers weren't ready. Not that many of them could get the ball down to second quickly, and not many throws came in low and on the bag. But with more players running in the last years, the young catchers are ready. They·can all throw and welcome the challenge of cutting down the top base runners."

"Challenge." That's a word with which Lou
Brock is very familiar. He's known about it ever
since his childhood, when the primary challenge
was simply to survive.

Lou Brock was born on June 18, 1939, in El
Dorado, Arkansas. But when he was still very
young, his parents separated, and his mother
packed up the family's belongings and took her
children to Mer Rouge, Louisiana, a small town
some ninety miles southeast of El Dorado. Mrs.
Brock had relatives in Mer Rouge and figured she
could get work there more easily.

Since there were nine children in the Brock
family, it wasn't easy for Mrs. Brock or for Lou
and his brothers and sisters. Lou's childhood filled
him with thoughts and images that were not only
difficult to overcome, but also left him with scars
that may never totally heal.

"You grow up insecure about everything," he
once admitted. "You grow up ashamed of your
mouth, ashamed of your nose, ashamed of your
skin. It takes a long time to overcome that."

Being black and poor—and living in a small
southern town—helped formulate these images on
Lou's mind, as it did with many other black
youngsters. They had no idea of what the world
was really like.

"When I was a kid that's the way I thought everybody lived," Lou says. "I didn't know there
was such a thing as a steady job. I thought everybody had a job for a day or two and got another
one."

It was largely that way for Mrs. Brock and
many of her friends and relatives. They did what-

ever work they could to support their families. As
Lou remembers:

"My mother did what all black women did to
support their children. She scrubbed floors and
cleaned up garbage."

Unpleasant memories, surely. But no more unpleasant than life itself was in Mer Rouge. It was
a hot, dusty town with not much to do during the
long summer months, as well as the rest of the
year. The boys played some ball, but went about
it half-heartedly. There was nothing and no one
to motivate them. They just kind of drifted
aimlessly from one thing to another, trying to find
a small measure of fun and something that would
hold their interest.

School didn't do much in that area. Lou
remembers how it was when he started.

"They make a big fuss about busing now," he
says. "Well, when I was a kid they bused us for
miles, way out of town, past a dozen white
schools, to the black school. Nobody talked about
that kind of busing."

But Lou remembers. He remembers watching
out the window of the bus and wondering what
life was all about. Despite his meager, almost
mechanical day-to-day existence, he sometimes
had visions of a better life.

"As a kid I wondered what life meant for me,
what life had in store for me," he recalls. "When I
looked at everything around me it wasn't a pretty
picture. I saw people unemployed, depressed. At
night sometimes I'd lay in bed and look up at the
stars, saying to myself: 'There has to be *something*
better for me. All right, how do I go about getting
it?' "

That was the problem. Getting it, whatever it was, seemed like a mere pipe dream. Wherever Lou thought of turning, the road seemed blocked by the poverty, depression, and general aimlessness of his small world. Then one day, when Lou was in junior high school and the boredom seemed worse than ever, he decided to have some fun. He rolled up a spitball and fired it at one of his friends. Only he missed. Instead, it hit his teacher smack in the forehead!

Lou's teacher was furious, but she knew that a tongue lashing—or even a physical beating—probably wouldn't have a lasting effect on the youngster. So she devised another kind of punishment. She sent Lou to the school library to do some research work on the careers of Jackie Robinson, Don Newcombe, Stan Musial, and Joe DiMaggio. Lou remembers what happened next.

"I didn't know a thing about baseball then, but I started reading anyway. I quickly found that these guys not only ran after a little white ball, but they got paid big money for it. So much money, in fact, that I couldn't even read the figures. So I took the book back to my class and asked the teacher what one of the numbers was. She told me it was one hundred thousand dollars!

"I couldn't believe it. One hundred thousand dollars—just for chasing the little white ball. From that day on I wanted to be a pro ballplayer. From that day on I knew how to get that something better. Through sport, the one time in a ghetto kid's life where everybody played by the same rules."

Lou hadn't played any serious ball before, and he had a lot of catching up to do. But as soon as he reached Union High School in Mer Rouge, he went out for baseball. He ended up playing four years of baseball and three of basketball at Union, and he really worked at it for the first time.

It didn't take long for Lou to learn he could excel. He was a guard and forward on the basketball team, pitched and played the outfield in baseball. He was fast even then, but since almost all of the players had real good speed, he didn't think about using it in any special kind of way. Besides, power was the name of the big-league game then, and Lou worked to be a stronger hitter.

The work seemed to be paying off. Lou never batted under .350 in high school, and as a switch-hitter his senior year he compiled a .536 batting average. Things were looking up. Maybe his dream wasn't so unreal after all.

Now came the time for a big decision. It wasn't a real difficult one to make. If Lou wanted to be a ballplayer and prepare himself for life at the same time, he'd have to go to college.

The tough part was finding a college that would offer him a scholarship. There was no way he could pay his own way. And in this area he found sports weren't equal. There were many more scholarships available for white athletes. The integrated schools always had more openings for whites, and the black schools didn't have that much money to pass around. Besides, there weren't as many black colleges to pick from.

Lou wrote letters and made applications to almost every school in the South. The responses were all negative. Only one held out any hope. That was Southern University, an all-black school located in Baton Rouge, Louisiana. Southern didn't make any promises to Lou but asked him to come down and visit the campus.

It was a 160-mile trip, and since Lou had no money, he was forced to hitchhike. But he got there and liked what he saw. More importantly, school officials liked him. They couldn't offer him a scholarship right then, but they did promise him work to help pay tuition.

Lou entered Southern in 1958. In the fall he started studies and a job as a part-time janitor and grasscutter. It was a rough grind, but Lou made it through to the spring and baseball time. Once again there was a test, and this time Lou almost didn't make it.

"I gave myself two weeks to make the team," he recalls. "I worked for two weeks hard as I could but the coach never took one look at me. I guess he was looking at the guys he knew and the ones who were on scholarship. But I stayed on anyway, kept practicing every minute I could. Then I lost my janitorial job. The little money I had was gone and to eat, I started visiting friends' houses right around mealtimes.

"On the field I tried to do everything to impress the coach. If I was playing left field and a ball was hit to right, I'd try to run it down. This kept up for another month. Then one day I just collapsed from exhaustion, right on the field."

His collapse forced the coach to notice Lou. The next time he got in the batting cage he knew the coach was watching. Weak as he was, he hit four straight balls over the fence. He was on the team.

There was a lot of learning for Lou that freshman year at Southern. He was still mastering fundamentals, since he had taken up the game later in life than most of the other boys. As a result he was a part-time player and hit under .200. But just being on the team was enough. It helped Lou straighten out his head and look to the future with optimism once more.

When he came back the next year, everything seemed to fall into place. Lou purposely took the hardest courses, concentrating on math (a subject area he felt could help him later in life). At various times during his stay at Southern, he wanted to be an architect or a teacher, but baseball changed all that.

Lou had scholarship money that year, and during the season he earned all Southwestern Athletic Conference honors with a .542 batting average. The improvement was amazing as more and more of Lou's natural talents became visible. He was expected to be even better in the 1961 season, but something happened to change all that: the Chicago Cubs offered the young outfielder a bonus of $30,000 to sign with them.

To Lou, who had known nothing but poverty all his life, it was a staggering sum. It was also a chance to pursue his dream. He now had the confidence and felt he could make it. So he quickly decided to leave Southern and sign with the Cubs.

The Cubs figured Lou would need some seasoning. They wanted to see what he'd do against other pros and assigned him to St. Cloud, Minnesota, in the Northern League. They figured if he did well during the 1961 season, they'd move him up a notch or two to one of their top minor league clubs. The only thing they didn't figure on was just how well Brock would perform.

In fact, Brock surprised the entire Northern League by burning it up from start to finish. He slammed out 181 hits in 501 at bats to win the batting title with a .361 mark. He also led the league in runs scored with 117, in doubles with 33, in put-outs with 277, and in hits with 181. In addition, he slammed out six triples, showed good power with 14 homers, and drove in 82 runs. And on top of all that he swiped 38 bases, using his exceptional speed and a little finesse. He played his first four major league games at the end of the 1961 season, and in 1962 he came to the majors to stay.

The Cubs did not have a powerhouse team when Brock joined them in 1962. There was room for young players, and Lou knew he had a good chance to crack the starting lineup. But although Lou knew he had speed, he thought he could make more of a contribution to the club through power.

"Maybe it was because there was so much emphasis on the home run then," he recalls, "and that's where I thought the money was. Or maybe it was because everyone had speed on my Southern University teams. But when I came to the majors, I really didn't think of myself as a base stealer. I felt I had good power and had always batted clean-up, or in one of the other power spots, so stealing bases wasn't on my mind at all."

But making good was on Lou's mind. He was so determined to stick in his first shot at a major league job that he put a lot of extra pressure on himself. A former teammate, pitcher Larry Jackson, remembers young Lou well.

"Lou just wasn't at all relaxed when he first

came to the Cubs," said Jackson. "He was so tense that it seemed as if he'd break out in a big sweat just putting on his uniform. He was making it even tougher for himself. And there were still things he had to learn. He knew the mechanics of sliding, for instance, but didn't always know when to start his slide. Sometimes he'd slide late and tear the bag right out of the ground. He was still finding out how to play the game."

Lou was also having trouble in the outfield. His great speed made up for some other deficiencies, but he had some trouble picking up base hits and making a quick decision on where to throw the ball.

Yet he had enough natural ability to see considerable action. Playing mostly right field, Lou was in 123 games as a rookie. The stats weren't bad. He batted .263 with 114 hits in 434 at bats. He had 24 doubles, 7 triples, 9 homers, and 35 RBIs. With his speed he swiped 16 bases, but it wasn't a real part of his game.

The next year was more of the same. Brock was a regular, appearing in 148 games, and helped his team. Only the team was never in contention for the league title, so there wasn't really any pressure on the players. So from that standpoint, Lou didn't really improve, because his statistics were nearly the same as his rookie year. He hit just .258 with 9 homers and 37 RBIs. He managed 24 steals, but he also struck out 122 times.

His problems in the field continued. One rival player said, "Every ball hit toward Brock is an adventure," and an opposing manager claimed, "Brock double-dribbles everything hit his way." Some of the writers and fans of the Cubs wondered if Brock would ever improve or whether he'd be just another ballplayer with good speed and an equal penchant for making mistakes.

Brock must have been wondering as well. After all, once he dedicated himself to baseball and became established in the game he had always been a star—in high school, college, and his one season in the minor leagues. It had been almost too easy. Then suddenly, when given his chance in the bigs, he was blowing it. And when the 1964 season started the same way, Lou's mind began to boggle.

"I was down," Lou confessed. "I was confused about everything, and the more I got confused, the more I tried to analyze the situation, the more I thought about it. And that just added to the confusion."

In mid-June of 1964, Lou was again hovering around .250. He wasn't really contributing much to the Cub cause. He had only 2 homers and 14 RBI's in 215 at-bats, and had stolen just 10 bases. His leading statistic was his 14 errors in the outfield, which seemed to indicate his ineptitude on the picket line was growing worse. No wonder Lou was down. Yet neither he nor anyone else could know then that in just a few short months he would be the central figure in one of the most fantastic turnarounds in baseball history.

Lou certainly could not be considered a hot piece of baseball property in June of 1964. Yet there was a veteran baseball man very much interested in him. That was Johnny Keane, manager of the St. Louis Cardinals, a team then embroiled in a race for the National League pennant.

The Cards had a sound team, but Keane felt

they were a player away from being outstanding. The need was for an outfielder, someone who could bat near the top of the order and create some action on the bases. At first glance it would seem that Brock had the raw ingredients, but he hadn't proven himself under fire. Yet Keane recalled a Cubs-Cards game earlier in the season when Brock had hit a hard grounder to third and had beaten a perfect throw to first. It was the kind of speed the Cardinal skipper was looking for. And on June 15, 1964, a trade was made that had everyone in St. Louis and Chicago buzzing.

The Cards announced that they had acquired Lou Brock in return for former 20-game winner, Ernie Broglio. Fans in both cities were vocal about it. Cardinal fans were disappointed; their team had traded a proven pitcher for an error-prone outfielder who batted .263 as a rookie and had gone downhill since. At the same time Club fans thought they had found a pitcher who would bring many victories to the Windy City.

But it didn't quite work out that way. Manager Keane told Brock he'd play every day and installed him in left field and in the second spot in the batting order. Suddenly, an amazing change came over Lou Brock.

Playing for a contending team and knowing what his role was expected to be, Lou warmed to the task. He knew the Cards wanted his speed to get things started, to ignite rallies, to get on base and upset the opposition, to add another dimension to the St. Louis attack. And as soon as he realized this, he did some thinking and went about making an adjustment.

"When I first came to the majors, I still felt that

power hitting was where the money was," Lou admitted. "But after a while I realized that power wasn't enough. You have to have *consistent* power, and I knew I didn't have the physical makeup to be a consistent long-ball hitter. So I had to make a choice. Do I go and try to develop myself as a powerhitter or do I become a pest on the basepaths?

"I didn't really make a final decision until I was traded to the Cards. Then I took inventory of myself all over again, and that's when I became a base runner."

Not that Lou didn't have power. While still with the Cubs he once hit a home run into the centerfield bleachers of the old Polo Grounds in New York. The blast had to travel more than 460 feet, making Lou one of a rare handful of players to hit a homer in that distant no-man's land. But it wasn't enough to produce thirty to forty homers a year, and by 1964, Lou knew it. So he soon concentrated on developing the other phases of his game, harnessing the long-dormant talents concealed within his lithe body.

Once he began concentrating on base hits and getting on, Lou started pounding the ball with more consistency, and the hits came in droves. He forced himself to concentrate even more on studying the pitchers and their motions, and soon, whenever he had the chance, he started running— and making it. The stolen bases were coming, too, and the whole Cardinal attack seemed to come alive. Lou was providing the added dimension that Manager Keane had been looking for.

"It just took a few games for us to realize we did the right thing," Keane said. "Lou was a sparkplug right from the start. And he learned so quickly. Within a month he was as much a base-stealing threat as any player in the league."

The hits continued to come. Lou was a .300 hitter from the day he joined the team, and the Cards quickly surged toward the top of the league. By August, Brock was surging toward a .300 batting average, and that included his .251 with the Cubs.

Still, it all came down to the final weeks of the season. The Cards were playing well, but they trailed the Philadelphia Phillies by 6½ games with only 12 games left. It didn't look good, but no one expected a complete Philly collapse (the club dropped 10 straight games). At the same time the Cards kept winning, closing the gap and clinching the pennant on the final day of the season.

The team had made a great comeback, yet in a sense, its comeback had to rank behind that of Lou Brock. After joining the Cards in June, Brock spent the rest of the season as a .348 hitter, bringing his overall average up to .315. In addition, he reached the 200-hit plateau for the first time. He stroked out 30 doubles, 11 triples, and 14 homers during the season. He drove in 58 runs, 44 of them from the Cards. He scored 111 runs (81 of them for the Cards) and stole 43 bases. Of those steals, 33 came after he donned the Redbird uniform.

It was obvious to everyone concerned that Lou had become an entirely different ballplayer after the trade. He had given the Cards what they needed—a ballplayer who could get things started, a man who would get on base and then drive the pitcher to distraction with his base-running heroics. More often than not, Lou was at the hub of Redbird rallies; he was the catalyst that provided the spark for the other fine Cardinal hitters (Curt Flood, Ken Boyer, Bill White, Mike Shannon, and Tim McCarver). He fit in beautifully, and now he was an integral part of a championship team.

Then came the World Series, and here the Cards had a tough nut to crack. They'd be facing the New York Yankees—the Yankees of Mantle, Maris, Tresh, Pepitone, Ford, Richardson, Kubek, Howard, Stottlemyre, etc. Injury and age would begin to take their toll on the Yanks the following year, but 1964 represented the Bombers' fifth consecutive American League pennant and they were heavy favorites to win the Series.

It was a hard-fought Series from start to finish. The Yanks knew it wouldn't be easy when the Cards bombed them, 9-5, in the opening game. During that game, the Yanks also lost the services of ace pitcher Whitey Ford, who developed a sore arm, for the remainder of the series. But the New Yorkers came back behind Mel Stottlemyre to take the second game, 8-3, beating Card ace Bob Gibson in the process.

The teams split the next two, the Yanks winning number three, 2-1, and St. Louis taking the fourth, 4-3. So far, it had been a frustrating series for Lou. He had a single, a double, and two RBI's in the first game; but then he went hitless in the next three. Being a young player, three hitless games could have finished him for the rest of the Series.

Fortunately, Lou wasn't that kind of player. He

had two hits and an RBI in game five as the Cards won behind Gibson, 5-2. The Yanks bounced back to win the sixth, 8-3, but Lou was the Cardinal star with three hits. Now it all boiled down to a seventh and final game. Mel Stottlemyre would pitch against Bob Gibson.

The game was scoreless for three and one-half innings. Then, in the bottom of the fourth, the Cardinals broke the ice. Lou singled in the middle of a three-run rally. In the next inning he started another three-run outburst with a long home run into the right-field stands. The Cards had a 6-0 lead. The Yanks cut this lead in half when Mantle belted a three-run homer in the sixth, but Gibson and his teammates hung on, winning the game and the Series, 7-5.

It had been an amazing season for Lou Brock. He had started the season as just another player for the Cubs and had finished it as a .300-hitting star for the Cardinals. In the Series he proved it was no fluke, batting an even .300 with 9 hits in 30 trips. He also had 5 RBI's in 7 games. In one year, Lou was on the top of the baseball world.

Brock was now confident of his job and himself. The sweet smell of success had touched him and stayed with him. He wanted to stay on top, and that meant working even harder to harness his natural talents. He started work right away in the spring. Even the exhibition games were important to him now, because he was always watching, studying every move every pitcher made.

When he got on base—even in an exhibition game—he began testing, experimenting, and learning just how far he could get off the bag and how to pick just the right moment to make his move.

At the plate he concentrated on hitting the ball to all fields—making contact, bunting, and doing everything that would make him more of a threat. When he was working out on his own, he practiced his starts, his acceleration, his sprinting, and his sliding. He remembered how little he'd improved during his years with the Cubs. He didn't want that to happen again.

And it didn't. During the next two seasons Lou firmly established himself as a consistent star and a dependable player who made things happen. His batting averages in 1965 and 1966 were .288 and .285. He had 16 homers and 69 RBI's one year, 15 homers and 46 RBI's the next. His stolen base totals were 63 and 74, beginning his string of 50 or more steals per year, as he quickly perfected his running techniques.

If Brock had any weakness it was in the field, where he was still sometimes prone to error. But with his speed, he also caught up with balls that other outfielders couldn't reach. Because of his aggressive play he sometimes gambled in the outfield. This led to miscues but also to potential great plays, and since he didn't make as many errors as in his Cub days, no one really complained.

At the plate Lou was becoming a complete hitter. Unlike many other base stealers, who tend to be strictly singles hitters, Lou was a threat to hit the long ball. He saw this clearly as an advantage.

"A pitcher will challenge a good base runner more often because he wants to keep him off the basepaths," said Lou. "But because they know I can hit it out, I'm not challenged quite as often."

Pitcher Claude Osteen, a crafty left-hander

then with the Dodgers, concurred about Lou's
skills at bat:

"Lou has no specific weaknesses up there, and
you just have to mix up your pitches and hope for
the best. If he gets on, he has so many different
moves and so much speed, it's almost impossible
to contain him."

The respect for Brock was growing every year.
However, the Cards slipped back in 1965 and
1966 (yielding the N.L. crown to the Dodgers),
but after the 1966 season, Dodger pitching ace
Sandy Koufax retired and the pennant was up for
grabs once more. And the Cards were one of the
top contending teams.

And as usual, with the pressure on and a good
pennant race in the works, Lou Brock was at his
best. He hit .299 in 1967, garnering 206 hits in
689 at bats. He was in the lineup day in and day
out. He also had his best power year, slamming
out 21 homers and driving home 76 runs. He
scored 113 times and swiped another 52 bases.
With a performance like that, it wasn't surprising
that he helped the Cardinals to another National
League pennant. This time St. Louis would be
facing the Boston Red Sox in the World Series.

Before the series started, one Red Sox scout
gave his evaluation of the opposition:

"The key to the series for us is stopping Brock.
He's the hub of their attack, the one who gets it all
going. If he gets a single, it's as good as a double,
and no one likes to see a man on second right off
the bat. If we can keep Brock off the bases, we've
got a great shot at winning."

There was one big question mark for the Cards.
Their pitching ace, Bob Gibson, had been out of

action with a broken leg from June 15 to September 7. Gibson had worked himself back into shape, but there was still a question of whether he could take the grind of perhaps three series starts. But Gibson was on the mound for game one, facing Boston's Jose Santiago. Red Sox ace Jim Lonborg, a 22-game winner, needed another day of rest after pitching the pennant-clincher on the last day of the season; he would be held for game two.

Gibson and Santiago matched serves for two innings. Then in the third, a familiar pattern emerged. Lou Brock hit a single. Then Curt Flood doubled, Brock taking third. Brock then sped home as Roger Maris grounded out. Pitcher Santiago surprised everyone by clouting a homer in the bottom of the inning to tie it. It stayed that way until the seventh when Brock came up once more.

Once again Brock slapped a base hit to the outfield. He danced off first, watching Santiago. Then he was off. Catcher Russ Gibson fired to second, but it was too late. Brock had his first series steal. A minute later it was evident just what a potent weapon the steal was. Brock breezed to third on an infield out and then scored on another infield out. Without the steal the run wouldn't have come home. The Cards took the game, 2-1, with Brock scoring both runs.

The second game was a different story. The Red Sox applied rule number one: they stopped Brock. In fact, Jim Lonborg stopped nearly everyone, pitching a brilliant one-hitter as the Sox won, 5-0; and evened the series. The series now moved to St. Louis, where the fans hoped their heroes would get rolling again.

First inning, Brock was up. Itchy from his hitless second game, Lou swung from the heels and drove a triple to right center. Flood followed with a single, and the Cards were on the board. A two-run homer by Mike Shannon made it 3-0 in the second. The Sox got one off Nelson Briles in the sixth, but then Brock went to work again.

This time Brock showed his speed by beating out a bunt. He danced off first, and when a pickoff throw went wild, he raced all the way to third. He then scored on a single by Maris. Each club got one more run, and the game ended up a 5-2 Cardinal win.

The fourth game was over before it began. Brock started it with another single; this was followed by a Flood base hit. Maris doubled both men home, and before the inning ended, the Redbirds had four runs. They got two more later, and Bob Gibson breezed past the Sox with a five-hit shutout. It was now 3-1, and the Series seemed to be in the bag.

In the next game Lonborg took the mound, and once again he applied his formula for success. Pitching brilliantly for a second time, the big right-hander stifled Brock and the Cards by pitching a three-hitter and winning a 3-1 victory.

Back in Fenway Park, the Sox had new life. They gambled with a young pitcher, Gary Waslewski, who held the Birds long enough for the Sox bats to go to work. Boston won it, 8-4, to tie the Series at three-games each. Brock had two hits and another steal, but this time his club lost. Now it was down to the final game. The Cards had Gibson, ready after three days rest, while Boston would have to gamble with Lonborg, who had been brilliant but would be pitching with just two days rest.

The game was scoreless for two innings, as the capacity crowd at ancient Fenway screamed on every pitch. But knowledgeable people in the press box didn't think it would last long.

"Lonborg's laboring," one writer said. "He's not throwing with the same smooth motion he had, and his fastball doesn't have the good hop."

Most of the others nodded in agreement. They also agreed that Gibson looked as sharp as ever and was flipping the ball up with a loose, effortless motion. Gibby was one of baseball's great competitors. If a team was going to get him, they usually had to do it early. Given a lead in the late innings, he usually got tougher and tougher, like most of the great ones. And the fire in Gibson's eyes was burning after just two.

In the third inning Lonborg's magic spell came to an end. A triple by weak-hitting Dal Maxvill started it. Singles by Flood and Maris and a wild pitch accounted for the first two runs. Then in the fifth the Redbirds struck again. First, pitcher Gibson aided his own cause with a home run. Then Brock rapped another single. Sensing the kill, he promptly stole second and then third. The unnerved Lonborg gave up a sacrifice fly to Maris, and it was 4-0.

Three more runs in the sixth settled the issue. Gibson weakened momentarily in the fifth and eighth, giving up a single tallies; but he pitched out of trouble to notch his third series win, 7-2, and to give the world's championship to the Cards.

His great pitching earned Gibson the MVP title

for the Series, but Lou Brock was right behind. Brock had a tremendous series, collecting 12 hits in 29 at bats for a .414 average. He also swiped 7 bases, erasing any doubts that he was now the premier base stealer in the majors.

The Cards continued to roll in 1968. Lou's stats fell off slightly, to a .279 average with just 6 homers and 51 RBI's; but he swiped 62 bases and was still the catalyst in many Redbird rallies, as the Cards took another N.L. title. So it was back to the Series, this time against the Detroit Tigers and their 31-game winner, Denny McLain.

But the Cards had Gibson again. Healthy all year, he had turned in a super season, winning 22 games, losing 9, and compiling a record-breaking 1.12 earned run average. When Gibson shut out the Tigers and whipped McLain, 4-0, in the opener, the pattern seemed to be established.

Still, it was the World Series, and the fall classic often produces unlikely heroes. In game two, the Tigers number-two pitcher, Mickey Lolich, handcuffed the Cards, 8-1, to even it up. The Cards took the third game, 7-3, as Brock starred with 3 hits and 3 stolen bases. Gibson then whipped McLain again, pitching brilliantly in a 10-1 Cardinal win. It was now 3 games to 1, and looked locked in. Brock had three more hits in that game, including a homer, a steal, and four RBI's. He was playing more brilliantly than ever.

Lolich came back to whip the Cards, 5-3, in game five, despite three more Brock hits, including a pair of doubles. The Tigers still had life though, and they finally got a strong game from McLain, who won game six easily, 13-1, as the

Tigers produced a ten-run third inning. Brock had just one hit in this one.

So it came down to a seventh game once again. Both teams had their best pitchers ready. It was Gibson against Lolich. The Cards were favored.

For six innings the game was a classic pitching duel. Neither pitcher budged. Then, in the top of the seventh, the Tigers came to life. With two out Norm Cash and Willie Horton each singled. Then Jim Northrup slammed a drive to center. Curt Flood, one of the best outfielders in the business, lost the ball among the white shirts of the huge crowd, giving Northrup a two-run triple. Bill Freehan then singled, and the Tigers had a three-run lead.

Lolich made it stand up. Both clubs scored in the ninth, but the Tigers won it, 4-1, coming back from a 3-1 Series deficit to take all the marbles. Lolich's third victory gave him the MVP award. Lou Brock again finished second. Lou had had another great Series, with 13 hits in 28 at bats for a .464 average. And once again he had stolen 7 bases, walloped 2 homers, and driven in 5 runs. But his performance didn't matter to him. His team had lost. And as with all the great ones, winning always comes first with Brock.

To everyone else, Brock was always a big winner. Though the Cards faltered during the next several seasons, Brock seemed to improve with age. From 1969 to 1973, Brock's batting averages were .298, .304, .313, .311, and .297. Each year he came to bat well over 600 times, and he had between 193 and 202 hits in each of those seasons. And of course, he was over the 50-steal mark each time.

Respect for Brock continued to grow in all corners of the baseball world. Hall of Famer Ted Williams, not a man usually given to compliments, said:

"Lou Brock is one hell of a base stealer. And he's even more effective because he gets the pitcher and catcher and the rest of the infield all on edge worrying about his stealing a base."

"He's the only base stealer who can actually outrun the little white ball," said Mets pitcher Jerry Koosman.

"How do you deal with the guy?" asked Bob Skinner, a former teammate of Brock's and now a coach. "You can't walk him, because when you do, it's like giving him a double. Whatever you try, he always seems to be creating winning situations, whether by hitting the long ball or bunting, or getting on base by making the other team hurry the play."

A former major league first baseman, frustrated by years of trying to hold Brock close and then watching him steal second, still found it hard to work up any animosity toward him:

"Lou never seems as intense as, say, Maury Wills. Maury would get on first and never say a word. You were the enemy, and he was concentrating on getting to second. Lou is different. He'll smile and say hello, maybe ask you about yourself or your family. But as soon as he's ready ... bam ... he's gone."

Brock's own manager, Red Schoendeinst, summed it up easily: "Lou Brock is just the most exciting player in baseball!"

It was Brock's outwardly cheerful nature and quick smile that led a writer to call him "the congenial superstar," a distinction he earned by his cooperative nature with the press and fans. But Brock's smile was something of a mask, too, as he would readily admit.

"People see me smiling when I'm on the field," he said. "But they don't always understand it. They don't know I smile the broadest when I'm the angriest."

Brock also has some definite ideas about sport and the athlete's responsibility to the public and to himself.

"Sport is current," he says. "People don't really come out to cheer for a Bob Gibson, a Lou Brock. They come out to cheer for the sport. People have been cheering these sports for years and years. My role is to play; their role is to cheer. The day after I retire there'll be someone else sliding into second base. And they'll be cheering just as hard."

In a sense, Brock has never received the widespread recognition that other stars, even some lesser ones, have gotten. This bothers him, though he's been mollified somewhat in recent years by a salary well over the $100,000 mark. He also knows that his peers—his teammates and others—are well aware of his presence on the field:

"When the chips are down, the ballplayers know what I can do to make this club a winner."

Brock's years in the game have helped him formulate a life style, a kind of philosophy that governs his actions. And as the years passed, the private Brock slowly became known to the public audience.

"Money per se doesn't turn me on anymore," he said a few years ago. "A lot of athletes are on ego-trips, *thing* trips. When I see a rookie making

$14,000 wearing a $200 suit, and driving an $8,000 car, I ask him: 'Why do you want to pretend you're something you're not?' He tells me: 'The public wants me to live up to a certain image, I gotta look like a pro.' I tell him: 'Baby, you're a fool. You should be wearing *jeans*.' "

In a sense, Brock has come full circle from his poverty-stricken childhood:

"My dreams don't center around getting more money. The more money I get, the more I want to get back to what I had to give up to make it: the simple life, the normal life.

"And the other side of the ego trip—fame—that doesn't turn me on, either. I've got a friend, a great ballplayer who's washed up. He should quit, but he can't. It's not the money—he has plenty already. It's the women, the road trips, the clubhouse, the fans, the spotlight. Baseball isn't just his livelihood anymore; it's his *life*.

"Well, the day I lose the touch, believe me, I'll quit. I'll retire. Retire, retire!"

Brock may not be obsessed by money, but he knows that life is infinitely easier when money isn't a constant worry. So he wants to be comfortable without having his life controlled by money and the desire or need to make more. He has solved this problem by making sound and long-lasting investments. He explains:

"Investing is a hobby with me, and that way I can enjoy it. I try to keep my investments diversified. I screen offers, I seek out things and decide whether it makes sound economic sense for me to get involved in them. During the offseason I travel a lot, do things like going to meetings, seminars, and investigating the politics involved in each venture. I get just as much satisfaction out of investing as I do out of baseball."

It all started with a flower shop, in which Lou posed on television for a Yellow Pages commercial. But since then he has become involved in, as he says, "more sophisticated" things. Brock isn't making the mistake of so many athletes. He's preparing for his future now, while he's still on top. So many stars wait until retirement to plan, only to find that their name no longer has the magic it did when they were in their athletic prime.

But at the same time, Lou Brock hasn't lost sight of his origins. He has always been interested in helping youngsters. Around 1965 he was the guest speaker at the Tandy Boys Club in St. Louis. After he finished speaking, someone told him the club was almost bankrupt. Lou didn't want to see all those kids lose a good thing, so he went on a speaking tour of his own just to raise some money for the club. And he didn't stop there. He took such a continuing active interest in the club that before long it was renamed the "Lou Brock Boys Club."

"Lou's the kind of guy who doesn't showcase the things he does for others," said Bill Alpine, who was a club director. "Let me give you an example. One day a box of trophies just turned up, enough trophies to last us at least five years. There was a little note in the box. 'From a friend,' it read. We just smiled and shook our heads. You know, as if to say, 'Well, Lou did it again.'"

Bill Alphin went on to say that it wasn't so much a matter of money, it was also the time Lou gave to the club. "It's just unbelievable when Lou comes in there. The kids just go wild."

As usual, Brock has given a great deal of thought to his role at the Club and in helping youngsters.

"There are a number of reasons why I'm dedicated to the Boys Club," he said. "One is the memory of my own childhood. Like so many other kids, I was basically uninformed. I could have gone in either direction, good or bad. People sometimes forget that baseball is a game of decisions. The kid has to learn how to make decisions. Sport teaches him to be decisive, and I think it can carry over into life.

"I also believe an athlete can get a kid's attention when a non-athlete can't. I remember when I was a kid, people were always telling me a lot of different things, warning me against this, suggesting that. But very little of that advice really registered because I was usually not paying attention.

"It was that way when I first started playing baseball. My high school coach was always lecturing me about hitting, running, throwing, all that stuff. But I never really gave a second thought to the things he was saying. Then one day Hank Aaron came into run a baseball clinic. He was the first pro athlete I'd ever seen. He started saying all the same things my coach had been saying for years, and all of a sudden they made sense. So it was because a pro said them that I suddenly became highly motivated. And that's the way it is with a lot of kids. This is the kind of thing that triggered my involvement with kids. I started out with the idea of giving them someone to identify with the way I identified with Aaron."

Lou also realizes that good advice is essential to the mature man, and he knows that many of his fellow pros have been victims of bad or wrong advice.

"Most athletes need advice when they turn pro," says Brock. "So the question becomes where do they get it? Usually the hangups begin when they go to their friends, because friends aren't qualified to give the athlete the kind of help he needs. Some go to agents, who can acquire money for them but have no special expertise on how to retain that money. That's the problem with the athlete—not how to get money, but how to hold onto it.

"And that makes good advice all the more essential for the black athlete. He must realize there isn't going to be a job waiting for him at the end of his career. So he can't allow himself to think in terms of 'job.' He has to create his own job, make himself independent."

Lou Brock has done this with his investments and business interests. He has created, through hard work and intelligence, a place for himself in the world once his playing days are ended.

But as of early 1974, there was no indication that his playing days were nearing any kind of end. In fact, he was off and running right from the start, and his stolen-base pace was so high that people were already looking twice. Brock had had a few self-doubts at the beginning of the 1973 season. But after receiving a vote of confidence and encouragement from Maury Wills, he began running the bases like a twenty-one-year-old. And at age thirty-five, he was still finding new ways to turn situations to his own advantage.

One catcher who gave Brock trouble for years was Jerry Grote of the New York Mets. As Brock has said, Grote is "quick out of the box, has a powerful arm, and always seemed to have a sixth sense about my stealing." So, for a time, Brock rarely tried to steal when Grote was catching. Then, one day in early 1974, things changed.

"Grote walked past me before a game, and I said hello to him," Lou recalls. "He either didn't hear me or was ignoring me so I said hello a second time. Again he didn't answer. So I screamed at him, *Hello Grote!* That seemed to bother him, and he was still upset about it when I came to bat. So when I got on I began screaming again. *Grote! Grote! Grote!* He wanted me to go, of course. So I went. And I finally beat him. Since that day I've run at about a ninety-percent efficiency against him."

Brock has always maintained, however, that he runs to win ballgames, not for records, and that claim would be difficult to dispute. But like most top base runners, Lou has a special kind of antipathy toward first base.

"First base is nowhere," he says, "and most times it's useless to stay there. On the other hand, second base is probably the safest place on the field. When I steal second, I practically eliminate the double play, and I can score on almost anything hit past the infield."

Brock continued to prove his point by stealing second at every opportunity. By the time the team had played 56 games, roughly one-third of the schedule, he had stolen 40 bases. People were be-

ginning to talk about his making a run at Wills'
record. As usual, he was hitting above the .300
mark, which put him on base often enough to
have a shot. (A .250 or even a .280 hitter simply
isn't on first base often enough to break the stolen
base mark.)

By the time the team had played half its games,
Brock had 50 steals. By August 1, he had 66,
though some thought his pace was slowing, that
his age was finally beginning to take its toll. But
in a weekend series against the Phils, he swiped 8
bases in 9 attempts, giving him 74 steals in 109
games, and talk of a record began anew. A further
advantage was that the Cardinals were in a pennant race for the first time in years, and everybody knew that Lou Brock always played his best
when the chips were down.

When Brock got steal number 90 in the team's
hundred and thirtieth game, it became obvious
that only an injury or other form of catastrophe
could prevent him from smashing the mark. The
publicity came in increasing waves, and more
people than ever were becoming aware of Lou's
great talents.

Then, in September, came some added, unex-
pected pressure. Both Brock and Cardinal rookie
centerfielder Bake McBride, received a letter
threatening their lives. The letter was filled with
racial slurs and written by a man who claimed he
was terminally ill and had nothing to live for. He
said he was going to shoot both Brock and
McBride right at the ball park.

Star ballplayers sometimes receive crank letters
but this one had more of a true ring to it, and

both outfielders were put under twenty-four-hour guard.

"I can't say this doesn't bother me," admitted Lou. "Whenever someone threatens to kill you it's real; the fear is there. Both Bake and I have got to try to forget about it."

Fortunately, the threat was never anything more than that, and Brock continued to run. He got steal number 100 against the Mets on September 6; he then tied and broke the record in the same game, against the Phils, on September 10.

"I never thought it would happen," admitted Lou, "but now that it did I'm glad it's over. I can't really say I care about records because I'm not on an ego trip. I just steal to win. But maybe when I'm seventy-five I'll care."

The old record holder, Wills, admitted *he* cared, and had mixed emotions when Brock set the new standard.

"I always felt it was my record," said Wills, "and I didn't think anyone would approach it so soon, not even in my lifetime. I don't think anyone looks forward to seeing his own record broken. So, honestly, I was hoping he wouldn't do it, but once he got around eighty it became very obvious. And don't get me wrong. I never wished Lou any tough luck. My hat's off to him."

More recognition soon came. The late Casey Stengel called Brock one of the four best base runners he'd ever seen, citing Ty Cobb, Max Carey, and Wills as the other three. And by the time Brock finished (with 118 steals, a .306 batting average, 194 hits, and 104 runs scored), his brilliance was being written about all over the country.

"The shame of it is," wrote one scribe, "that the Cards didn't win the pennant. Because then the entire country would have had the pleasure of seeing Lou Brock perform in another World Series, where his sheer artistry becomes more evident than ever."

But Brock didn't get full recognition. Steve Garvey of the Dodgers, who also had an outstanding year, won the National League's Most Valuable Player award, with Lou a close second. It bothered Lou, though he admitted that Garvey had had a MVP-type season, and since the Dodgers had won the National League pennant, the odds had been tipped in Garvey's favor.

Many people felt Lou deserved it. But at least his skills were now fully appreciated. Limited to just 136 games in 1975 because of some minor injuries, Lou nevertheless hit .309 and swiped 56 bases, giving him a lifetime total of 809 steals and putting him well within striking range of Ty Cobb's all-time mark of 892. That record could fall to Lou's flying feet in two years or so. And it could be the final goal of his great career.

Who would have thought it of the young, raw, unrefined kid who came up with the Cubs in 1962. For a while it looked as if his speed and talents would never be harnessed in the right direction. But as always, Brock accepted the challenge and became one of the most exciting and respected players of his generation. Perhaps it was the Mets' Bud Harrelson who best summed up the feeling toward Lou Brock around the entire league.

"I'm happy for Lou," said Harrelson. "He has done a lot for base stealers, and I root for him.

He's a good friend of mine. He's good for baseball. He's never shamed the game."

Lou Brock, king of the base runners, is truly a popular champion.

Rod Carew

When talking about baseball the easiest way to
start an argument is to claim that someone is the
best at something. Go over to any group of three
or four fans and say that this guy is the best
pitcher, that one the best outfielder, another the
best third baseman, and still another the most
feared slugger. Surely one or more of the group
will interrupt without hesitation, say "Hey, wait a
minute!" and proceed to give you his opinion,
which he will defend to the last.

And generally speaking there is plenty of room
for debate. The argument can go on and on, season after season, generation after generation, usually without resolution.

Down through the years such arguments have
raged. Who was the better hitter, Cobb or
Hornsby? the most feared power man, Ruth or
Gehrig? the better pitcher, Koufax or Marichal?
Sometimes more than two players are compared,
as in the Williams-Musial-DiMaggio debates of
the 1940s and the Mantle-Mays-Snider arguments
of the 1950s. Who do you think was the better
hitter, Aaron or Clemente? It goes on and on.

But there is one baseball argument that is rapidly becoming no argument at all. That's because just about all baseball people everywhere agree. The best pure hitter in baseball is Rod Carew, second baseman for the Minnesota Twins.

Johnny Bench may seem the best to some, especially when you're talking about homers and RBIs. Or how about Pete Rose, with his string of .300 averages and 200-plus-hit seasons? Rose is the most consistent. But the best pure hitter, the best at handling the bat, at knowing how to maneuver for base hits, and at compiling impressive batting statistics? With each passing year, more votes swing over to the Carew camp, and there aren't many holdouts left.

Prior to the 1976 season, Rod Carew had the highest lifetime batting average of any active player, .328, and it was rising. From 1973 through 1975, Carew had league-leading season averages of .350, .364, and .359. Combined with his .318 of 1972, these averages gave Carew four straight American League batting titles. He was the first to win that many batting titles in a row since Ty Cobb, who won his titles prior to 1920. Carew took the bat crown again in 1969, giving him five batting titles in all. Only five players in all of baseball history have more: Ty Cobb (12), Honus Wagner (8), Rogers Hornsby (7), Stan Musial (7), and Ted Williams (6). So Rod is traveling in some pretty fast Hall of Famer company.

There is one batting achievement that hasn't been accomplished in more than thirty-five years. No batter in either league has hit .400 over a season since Ted Williams slammed the ball at a .406 clip in 1941. Yet if you ask any player, coach, manager, sportswriter, or broadcaster which of today's players has the best chance of reaching that magical plateau, the answer is unanimous—*Rod Carew*.

This, in itself, indicates that Carew is considered the best pure hitter in the game. And for the past three seasons he has flirted with that .400 mark in the early months of the season—even as late as July. But it's perhaps the toughest of all batting marks, since the game, the pitching and the equipment have all changed, making it more difficult to reach the .400 mark. Almost all the .400 hitters appeared in the early days, from 1900 to the early 1920s. There were a few afterward but not many. In fact, before Williams hit .406 in 1941, the last was Bill Terry's .401 in 1930. So in the National League, the gap is moving close to half a century.

At the plate, Rod Carew has no weakness. He can handle any pitch and any pitcher. He can hit to any field at any time in any situation. And when he does go into an occasional slump, he usually breaks it by bunting. And he can bunt better than any other player in the majors. In fact, one year he beat out 25 of 37 bunts for base hits.

But Rod Carew didn't put on a major league uniform and promptly begin slamming hits all over the place, placing bunts to precise spots, and handling every pitch with relative ease. True, Rod has a large measure of natural ability. He hit .292 as a rookie in 1967 and was promptly named American League Rookie of the Year. That year and every year since, Rod Carew has been voted the starting second baseman on the American League All-Star team.

Yet from the time he came up to the Twins, Carew has been one of the hardest working players around. He takes batting practice incessantly, more than anyone else. He practices his bunting like a scientist, working for hours to perfect his technique by figuring the angles, the odds, the pitchers, everything.

Of course, when a player excels at one phase of the game, there is a tendency to criticise his play in other ways. So Carew works on his weak points too, claiming he isn't interested in just being a good hitter but in being a good "all around ballplayer." Thus, he's made himself into one of the game's best base runners, usually getting around 40 steals a year. In 1969 he really drove everyone nuts; he set a record by stealing home 7 times during the year.

Then they said he was a lousy fielder, pointing to a couple of years in which he made a large number of errors. Perhaps Carew is not a perennial Gold Glover, but he's worked to make himself into a good, solid second baseman.

The final rap against Carew was that he was just a Punch and Judy hitter with little run-producing power. But Rod always claimed that wasn't his job, not when the team had the likes of Harmon Killebrew and Tony Oliva hitting behind him. With Killebrew gone and Oliva limited to part-time duty as a designated hitter in 1975, Carew upped his power stats to 14 homers and a team leading 80 runs batted in. And he did it without sacrificing his batting average and while hitting in the number two spot in the order.

But baseball wasn't the only thing Rod Carew had to work on. Born and raised in Panama, he came to New York City as a teen-ager with a language problem and specializing in a sport that doesn't really go over big in the city. Thus when he came up, Rod was pretty much of a suspicious loner, very sensitive to kidding teammates, and shy with fans and reporters. He was often a solitary figure, taking batting practice alone and doing wind sprints and exercises after the rest of the team had ended workouts for the day.

It didn't help when the sports world at large learned that Carew, a black Panamanian had married a white girl who also happened to be Jewish. This prompted the sickies to creep out of the woodwork, and Carew received a bevy of hate mail and disparaging remarks at the ball parks around the league. This could have easily gotten the best of him; that is, if Carew's character wasn't basically strong and on very solid ground. Now, at age thirty and at the peak of his career, the slender Carew is very sure of himself and his life, his goals and aspirations, his place in the world. It's even come to the point where Rod has admitted that he has a chance to hit .400, something he never talked about in past seasons.

But to fully understand Rod Carew and his development into baseball's best hitter, it's necessary to go back to the beginning. It's not hard to understand why Carew is always moving on the ball field. After all, he got his start in life that way—he was born on a train.

Rod's family lived in Gatun, in Panama's Canal Zone, and when Olga Carew felt she was ready to give birth on October 1, 1945, she had to move fast. There was no hospital in Gatun, so she boarded a train that would take her to the hospi-

tal at nearby Colon. But she never made it. Young
Rod Carew arrived right on that train. Fortunately, there was a trained nurse in the same car
as Olga Carew, and then a doctor was located in
the other end of the train. The doctor's name was
Rodney Cline, so a grateful Olga Carew named
her infant son Rodney Cline Carew.

So it was back to Gatun, where Rod spent his
early years. The Carews lived in a poor section of
the town. Rod's father was a house painter and
worked very hard to provide for his wife and children. Rod remembers being poor but happy in
those early years.

"Mom and Dad always tried to provide for us,
even though we didn't have much money," he
says. "I was lucky in that I never wanted the so-
called luxury toys that other kids had. I didn't
care for owning things like bicycles. There was
just one thing that made me happy from as far
back as I can remember, and that was walking
around all day with a bat and glove."

This meant playing ball whenever he could,
whether it be a full game or just hitting flies with
two or three of his friends. Young Rod walked
from park to park looking for the action. Sometimes he just practiced hitting tennis balls when
he could find someone to pitch. Other times there
were no tennis balls, and they had to use big
wads of paper taped into a ball.

Baseball was extremely popular in Panama, as
it is in many Latin American countries, so the
young boys knew how to play the game. There
was an organized Little League there, and Rod
joined up as soon as he was old enough. That was
the first time he really played for a team.

The boys were also familiar with the major leagues in America, and had many of the same heroes as boys in New York, Chicago, and Los Angeles. All the papers carried scores of the big league teams and stories of the top players. Blacks and Latins were just beginning to appear in the majors when Rod was young, and before long he began to dream about playing there someday, too.

When Rod was sixteen there was a crisis in the Carew household. His parents were separating. Olga Carew decided to take Rod and his three sisters away from Gatun and to America. She had remained in touch with the nurse who helped deliver Rod on the train and was urged by her to come to New York City. So that's where the Carew family went in 1962.

"I remember the night we came into New York on the plane," Rod recalls. "I was awed looking down at the lights of the city. It was an impressive sight. But I soon found I didn't really like it in New York. I didn't enjoy the crowds. I liked to be by myself. I still do."

It wasn't easy for Rod to be deposited suddenly on the streets of New York. He had to learn things in a hurry. He knew that blacks sometimes had it rough, and since he spoke with a heavy Spanish accent, it was even harder for him to find new friends.

He went to George Washington High School in Manhattan, where he also kept pretty much to himself, though the few friends he had quickly tuned him in to the ways of the streets.

But school wasn't really his style. Before long he began realizing what so many black and Spanish youngsters find out, that there just weren't many opportunities open for him, especially if they had no real skills. Before long, his old dream returned, and he began walking the streets, as he had in Panama, bat and glove in hand, looking for some baseball action.

Unfortunately, baseball isn't a game that adapts to the pavements of the big cities, especially today, when there are fewer and fewer good places to play. There have certainly been some fine ballplayers from the cities, but they've generally had a tougher time making it than their country cousins. To make the point, George Washington didn't even have a baseball team, eliminating a primary outlet and developing ground. But Rod didn't quit. He kept on searching.

"I just kept scouting around until I finally found a sandlot team, the Cavaliers. They played most of their games in the Bronx, and their home field was a sandlot right next to Yankee Stadium. None of the players knew me, but they let me try out. I remember how surprised they were that I could hit a ball so far because I was pretty thin at the time."

But Rod's experience in Panama had paid off. Naturally, he quickly became a star of the Cavaliers, a team made up mostly of South and Central American players, who, like himself, had come to America from their homelands.

It was hard to imagine what happened next. Rod had come to this country in 1962, several months before his seventeenth birthday. In the spring of 1963, he had begun playing sandlot ball with the Cavaliers. The father of one of his teammates was a man named Monroe Katz. Katz

was what is known as a "bird dog." That means
he checked out local talent for a major league
scout, in this case Herb Stein of the Minnesota
Twins. Stein had a lot of respect for Monroe Katz,
and as soon as he heard about the young infielder
from Panama who could hit like the blazes, he
arranged a tryout.

The tryout took place in the summer of 1963,
just about a year after Rod came to New York.
And it took place in the legendary big ball park
next to the sandlot, Yankee Stadium. The Twins
were in town to play the Yanks, and Rod got the
chance to work out with the big club. He didn't
blow it. He showed he could handle himself
adequately in the field, but the thing that
impressed everyone most was his hitting. Standing relaxed and easy on the left side of the plate,
Rod begain stroking the ball to all fields. He
swung at everything, good pitches and bad ones,
and he was making contact, spraying the ball
with good authority. The more he hit, the more
players and coaches gathered around to watch. If
Rod was nervous he didn't show it. He just kept
hitting until someone told him to stop.

It didn't take the Twins' brass long to reach a
decision. Before the club left town they offered
Rod a contract, with a small bonus, and he
jumped at the chance.

"My head was swimming," he said. "I couldn't
believe this was happening to me. It seemed as if
I had just come to the United States with nothing
really going for me, and within a year I was in a
major league organization. I was nervous, I guess
scared, but I wanted to make good."

Rod was still young, and the team didn't want

to rush him. For 1964, they sent him to Melbourne, Florida, so he could play and learn in the Rookie League. There was a great deal of instruction, many drills, many practice sessions, and some ballgames (37 for Rod). But in those 37 games Carew showed his hitting was for real. Consistent from start to finish, he batted .325, with 40 hits in 123 at bats. Most of them were singles; there were just 5 doubles and 3 triples among them. But he drove home 21 runs and stole 14 bases. It was a good start, and for 1965, he was promoted to Orlando in the Florida State League.

The season at Orlando turned into a tension-ridden turning point for Carew. Not because of his play, which was improving. It was his relationship with his teammates that was causing the problem. For the first time Rod was thrown together with all the various types of men that make up a professional baseball team. They're all different, and they're not always proverbial nice guys. There are the kidders, the guys who fool around, and the jealous ones who begin to realize they're not going to make it and take it out on the others. Rod was still a relative newcomer to many American customs, and in a sense naive to the ways of many people. Before long, some of his teammates began getting to him.

A man named Bob Willis was the manager of the Orlando team in 1965. Willis had a tough exterior. He was short and stocky, and he looked as if he'd mixed it up a few times in his youth. But he wasn't all that tough on his players and gave them a pretty free rein, as long as they produced on the field. So, at first, Willis wasn't aware of what was happening.

"I was out on the field for practice one day in the middle of the year when I couldn't find Rod. I looked all over the place. Everyone was out there but Carew. Rod wasn't the type of guy to skip practice. In fact, he always practiced longer and harder than anyone, so I knew something must be wrong.

"Then my kid, who was our bat boy, comes running up to me all excited, shouting something about Rod being in the locker room packing his bags. 'He says he's going home!' my son shouted.

"Man, I almost panicked. The guy was hitting over three hundred, and I'd already been told that Mr. Griffith [Calvin Griffith, owner of the Twins] was expecting Rod to be his next superstar. So when I heard he was packing, I took off like I was shot out of a cannon. When I got to the locker room, there was Rod, cleaning out his locker. I didn't know what to say, so I just asked what he was doing, as if I didn't know.

" 'I'm going home,' he says. 'I'm quittin' baseball. I've had it.'

"So I said to him, 'Look, if you *walk* out, they'll *throw* me out. The owner will shoot me if I let you go.' "

Then the two sat down to talk. The problem was Rod's relationship to his teammates. He was a very sensitive young man, and according to Bob Willis, was interpreting many of the remarks made by teammates as racial slurs. The fact remains that Rod was one of the first black ballplayers at Orlando, and if history is any barometer, there was undoubtedly some resentment and some outright prejudice on the part of a few players.

Rod was also hitting over .300 for the entire season and had as good a chance as anyone of being brought up to the Twins. So there was also some jealousy. Rod remembers some of them yelling, "Blooper ball!" whenever he got a hit that wasn't a solid line drive. So it was a tense situation, one that made Rod pretty much of a loner. But he came to his senses and finished out the season. There was too much to lose, and walking out certainly wouldn't solve any problems.

Carew's statistics were encouraging this year. He had a .303 batting average in 125 games, including 133 base hits. This time he had 20 doubles, 8 triples, 1 homer, and 52 RBIs. He also burned up the Florida State League base paths with 52 steals. So on the field, Rod Carew hadn't disappointed anyone. He might have been brought up right then and there, but the Twins had a pennant-winning team in 1965 and decided to leave him in the minors for additional seasoning. So in 1966 he went to play for the Wilson team in the Carolina League.

The manager at Wilson was Vern Morgan, and it wasn't long before he realized that the talented Carew needed some special handling.

"Rod was quite moody when he first came here," said Morgan. "Maybe part of it was that he had spent the whole winter in the Marine reserves. And maybe another part of it was the experience at Orlando. I think both those things made him homesick, and the homesickness made him moody."

Morgan talked to Carew whenever he could,

trying to explain things to the youngster and encourage him to stay with it. There was still the fear within the Twins' organization that Rod might just pack up and leave. But finally, after hours of talk, which sometimes bordered on pleading, Manager Morgan seemed to crack the Carew barrier.

"Vern made sense," Rod remembers. "He kept telling me over and over that if I didn't make it to the big leagues I had wasted a lot of time. I'd be nowhere, he told me. Then he reminded me that while I was a good hitter and improving all the time, I was still making mistakes and was unsure in the field. And a lousy fielder can't make it in the bigs. So that was a start. From that point on, Vern and I worked very hard, as often as we could."

Morgan and Carew would often stay late at practice, and the manager would just keep hitting grounders at the second baseman. He hit them every way, fast, slow, to the right, to the left, at him, bouncers, grasscutters, and a few other kinds that defy description. Slowly, painfully, Rod's fielding improved. They even worked on Rod's hitting. Morgan watched the natural Carew stroke carefully. And whenever he thought he saw a minor flaw, the two men discussed it, and then worked on it.

Yet, on occasion, Rod still became depressed, discouraged, and dejected, and he talked about going home. In Vern Morgan's words, "He was his own worst enemy," and when he brooded, his batting average often dipped. Then one day an incident occurred which Vern Morgan says he'll never forget, for it changed everything. He remembers:

"We were playing in Burlington, North Carolina, and Rod was in one of his down periods. He suddenly said he didn't want to play. He said his foot was hurting him, but we both knew what the real trouble was. That was just an excuse. Anyway, we had a pitcher going that day who really needed a win. I don't remember exactly why, but he wanted that victory. And when he heard that Rod wasn't going to play, he became frantic. He ran into the clubhouse looking for Rod, who was sitting there, moaning over his foot. So the pitcher ran into the trainer's room and came back with some bandages and salve. Then he started pleading with Rod.

" 'Let me fix it for you,' he said. 'I'll bandage it up so you can play.'

"Well, he kept this up until Rod was forced to take him seriously. When he realized the pitcher wasn't kidding, he was stunned. The whole thing really made a deep impression on him. He went out there that day, got four hits, and won the game for us. And it was the last time he pulled the homesick number. After that, he was here to stay. He never refused to play again, because for the first time he saw that he was really wanted."

So Carew finished the 1966 season on a high note. He played in 112 games and batted a respectable .292, not as high as in past years but still good enough for the parent club to take a long look at him in the spring of 1967.

The Twins had been American League champs in 1965, but lost a hard-fought World Series to the Dodgers, 4 games to 3. They were a solid club

at most positions, led by slugger Harmon Killebrew, top-hitter Tony Oliva, shortstop Zoilo Versalles, and pitcher Jim "Mudcat" Grant. It wasn't
an old team, and the experts figured they'd be on
top for some time.

But in the next couple of years, several key
players inexplicably lost their touch. Shortstop
Versalles, the league's Most Valuable Player in
1965, stopped hitting completely and was
traded. Pitcher Grant, a 20-game winner in the
pennant year, never came close again. Sluggers
Bob Allison and Don Mincher stopped producing
consistently, while catcher Earl Battey, a steady
performer, simply began getting old. So when
Rod came around for the first time in 1967, the
club was ripe for some new faces.

The second baseman during the 1965 Series
was Frank Quilici, who later became the club's
manager. Quilici never proved to be more than a
good utility player, so when Rod began looking
sharp during spring training in 1967, he was
promptly installed at second, with Quilici moving
to third. The second base job was his. He had
made the big leagues in his first try. When the
1967 season opened, twenty-one-year-old Rod
Carew was standing out at second base for the
Minnesota Twins.

It was hard to figure what Rod's place in the
game would be then. He came up without much
advance notice, except for the Twins' officials who
had high hopes for him. But the league at large
wasn't expecting anything special. Just another
spray hitter without much power was the general
consensus.

It's necessary to look at a bit of baseball history

to fully appreciate the prevailing attitude toward the likes of a Rod Carew in 1967. To do this, it's necessary to return to the beginning, to the turn of the century, when major league baseball was in its embryonic state.

The game was decidedly different then, much of the difference dictated by the times as much as anything else. Ball parks were smaller, of course, but they were also much rougher (there were no smooth infields). The dirt was rocky and rough and was hard to play on. Astroturf, or an artificial surface, wasn't even a pipe dream of the most imaginative of men.

Then there was the equipment, most notably the gloves, which were small and flat. The gloves' purpose was just to protect the hands of the fielders. They were almost a hindrance instead of a help in picking up a ground ball. There were no deep self-sustaining pockets to make one-hand grabs and lunging stops automatic. Such plays came strictly through the merits of the individual fielders. So rule number one was that any ball—bouncer, grounder, or chopper—hit to the infield, had a good chance of somehow getting through.

The ball, of course, was made differently, and it simply didn't carry. It didn't leap off the bat and fly out to the far reaches of the ball park. In a sense, when hit, the ball just died. Hence, the era of the "dead ball." And although outfield fences were generally closer to the plate then, it still took a mighty wallop to hit one out. So the league's big "sluggers" might hit eight to ten homers a year, if they were lucky.

So where did that leave the good hitters? It left them with a attitude best exemplified by the leg-

endary Wee Willie Keeler, one of the best of the
turn-of-century batsman. Asked about his hitting
philosophy, Keeler answered quickly:

"I hit 'em where they ain't."

Today, that's one of the most famous lines in
baseball annals, a maxim that will live on as long
as the national pastime is played. But when
stated, it contained a barrelful of truths. The fine
hitters of the day were truly bat manipulators
who literally hit 'em where they ain't, deftly placing the ball between infielders, in the outfield
gaps, down the lines, bunting when they caught
the infielders deep, chopping it past them when
the infielders were in close. They rode with the
pitch, trying to make contact. Sometimes they intentionally swung down, blasting the ball right
down onto the rough dirt of the infield. Whereas a
two-base hit today is usually achieved on a hard
outfield shot, doubles then were often the result of
surprise tactical base running or of balls that died
on long outfield grass or hit a rock and skipped
past a fielder. Very few players uppercut the ball
or had thoughts of hitting high long drives to the
outfield. There was no percentage in doing that,
not if one wanted a base hit.

As a consequence, there were plenty of outstanding hitters in the first two decades of the
century, men who regularly hit in the upper .300s,
with the .400 average almost a yearly occurrence
by one or more players in either league. Shoeless
Joe Jackson once batted .408 and didn't win the
American League batting title. It sounds impossible, but it happened back in 1911, when a
player named Ty Cobb batted .420.

Ty Cobb, the Georgia Peach, is widely considered the best hitter of all-time. In 24 big league seasons, from 1905 to 1928, Cobb had a lifetime batting average of .367, a totally incredible figure. He batted over .400 three times and took 9 consecutive batting championships, from 1907 through 1915. Then after a year off (hitting only .371), he took three more batting titles. Cobb won his last batting crown in 1919, yet after that he had years of .389, .401, .378, and .357 without taking the crown.

Anyway, Ty Cobb is considered the epitome of the early bat handlers who could get a base hit in so many ways. He was a left-handed batter who kept his hands spread several inches apart on the bat, allowing for better control. He could slide his lower hand up, or drop his top hand down, depending on where he wanted to place the ball. And he changed his stance to fit the situation and to throw the opposition off balance. Ty was also a master bunter and base stealer. That was his game. Anything to win.

Ty Cobb believed that hitters weren't born, that they learned the art through trial and error and through constant practice. He felt that his kind of hitting was a purer form of baseball than swinging for the fences. And in his autobiography, completed shortly before his death in 1961, he wrote:

"Boys, strive to master the lost arts of a great game. Unless you dedicate yourself to that task now, as the old timers die off one by one, they will have vanished forever."

Ty had plenty of reason to pen those words. For in the early 1920s, the game of baseball began to change. It changed principally because of one man and because of the crowds he was able to attract by swinging the bat in a big, new way. When George Herman "Babe" Ruth unexpectedly shattered all existing records with 59 home runs in 1921, people saw exciting new possibilities for the grand old game. Suddenly, a new ball was coming out, a livelier one that jumped off the bats as if it had been shot from a cannon. Ruth was truly an extraordinary slugger, as was teammate Lou Gehrig. But before long other sluggers were coming along, and the home run became an integral part of the game.

The long ball probably reached its zenith in the 1950s and early 1960s. It was the beginning of the big money era, and the big money was being paid to the big men who could drive the ball a country mile. More home runs were being hit than ever before, and more players were considering themselves sluggers. Most of the top players of that day were the men who could put the ball in orbit with one swing of the bat—Mantle, Mays, Aaron, Killebrew, Robinson, Mathews, McCovey, Colivito, Howard, Hodges, Snider, Campanella, Stargell, and on and on. True, many of them were fine all-around players, but the emphasis was truly on the home run.

Then, gradually, in the 1960s, things began to change again. Players who knew they couldn't hit 50 home runs a year began to concentrate on other things. In 1962, Maury Wills of the Dodgers shocked the baseball world by stealing 104 bases, thus reviving an art that had been dormant for decades. Suddenly, young players everywhere began stealing once more.

And about that same time a player named Pete

Rose came up with the Cincinnati Reds and began banging base hits all over the lot. Rose wasn't just a little guy who got Punch-and-Judy hits. He was a stocky, powerful player who likened himself to a throwback of days gone by. Rose soon picked up the nickname of "Charlie Hustle," began attracting new fans, and then proclaimed:

"I'm going to be the first $100,000 singles hitter!"

Until then, the super big contracts were always reserved for the sluggers. Rose was the prime mover in changing all that.

So a new era began to dawn. Pirate outfielder Roberto Clemente was suddenly getting more recognition than ever before. He, too, disdained the home run for batting average, and people began to admit that he was every bit as much a superstar as sluggers Mantle, Mays, and Aaron. In the World Series of 1967 and again in 1968, one of the brightest stars was Cardinal outfielder Lou Brock, who had 25 base hits and 14 stolen bases in those two World Series and produced as much excitement as any slugger possibly could.

This brings us right back to the debut of Rod Carew. He had played his game the same way from the start. He knew he wasn't a slugger. Some others, including Brock, had to learn about themselves the hard way, but the new ball parks, with distant fences, taught the lesson quickly. And with Pete Rose earning the big money with his singles bat, others had hope and didn't try to alter their basic styles. Rod was one of them. As soon as he got to the big leagues, he went about working to perfect the things he did best.

It didn't all come together overnight, but Rod

was still plenty good during his rookie year. He
flirted with the .300 mark all season long, was
voted the starting second baseman on the All-Star
team at midseason, and finished with a .292
mark in 137 games (collecting 150 hits and surprising everyone with 8 homers and 51 RBI's).
He won the American League's Rookie of the
Year prize handily, and he seemed to be at the
beginning of a fine career.

The next year a few doubters emerged, because
Rod had his poorest season at the plate. He also
had a bad knee part of the year, which limited
him to 127 games. He also played on the bad
knee for a while and had the longest hitless streak
of his career. He recalls:

"I was 0-for-17 and really starting to press.
Then I hit a line drive and the outfielder almost
made a spectacular catch but dropped it. I had
9-for-10 after that and I was on my way."

Though Rod made the All-Star team again in
1968, he had an offseason, hitting just .273. It
was partly the bad knee and partly his unfamil-
iarity with the league and his need to work even
harder. Perhaps his confidence was still not what
it should be. But in 1969 he gave an indication of
what was to come.

This was the year Carew took his first batting
title, emerging from the pack to post a .332 average. Once again, minor injuries limited him to
123 games, but he still managed 152 hits in
458 at bats, including 30 doubles, 4 triples, 8
homers, and 56 RBIs. Being a free swinger he
walked just 37 times, and he swiped 19 bases.
But it was the steals that got him his first real bit

of solid notice. For of those 19 steals, 7 of them were steals of home.

"I would have had even more, but during the entire second half of the season whenever I got on third, the pitchers came to a stop position instead of taking the full windup. Since pitchers don't like to do this with a man on third. I can only hope I helped throw their timing off somewhat."

Despite his first batting crown and first taste of notoriety, Carew wasn't a completely happy man in 1969. Occasionally he still became depressed and tended to brood, and he still habored suspicions about some teammates, a few of whom had been on that Orlando team back in 1965. So he kept pretty much to himself and his reputation as a loner grew. But during that year, something happened that was to change Rod's life and actually put him to another kind of test. That was the year he met his future wife.

It seems like a simple enough thing on the surface; after all, Rod was at an age when many men get married. But there was a difference. Rod was at a nightclub one night when a man, trying to impress his date, walked over and told the girl he wanted her to meet Rod Carew.

"Rod who!" was, in effect, what the girl said. Her name was Marilynn Levy. She was white and Jewish. Rod, being black and a Latin, would seem to be at the complete opposite pole. But the two of them hit it off immediately and were soon seeing each other regularly.

"Marilynn didn't know anything about baseball when I first met her," Rod recalls. "And when she was told that I was a pro ballplayer, what some people call a 'star,' the news didn't impress her one bit."

In a sense, dating Marilynn created a potful of potential problems for Rod. Interracial dating and marriage is still frowned upon with varying degrees of belligerence, and he knew exactly what to expect. Yet he played better than ever on the field, taking his first batting crown, and in the offseason, his relationship with Marilynn became even more involved. Finally, they became engaged.

"At first, Marilynn's parents were very negative about us," Rod says. "Her mother didn't even want to meet me until one day when we were both invited to dinner at Marilynn's sister's house. It was the night we got engaged, and as it turned out, Marilynn's mother and I were both in for a surprise. We hit it off real well. The only thing she asked me that night was, 'Please, take care of my little girl.'"

Rod and Marilynn were married in early 1970, and Rod says he never personally thinks about their union in terms of black and white.

"I love my wife," he has said. "We enjoy each other's company; we understand each other. I never think of my wife as being white. I just think of her as being a woman."

Unfortunately, there were people who didn't see it that way, and Carew admits that he's received his share of obscene letters, especially a few years after the marriage when it was learned that he was studying the Jewish religion.

"There are a lot of sick people in the world," Carew said. "I always knew people would say there are two strikes against me. I'm a black man who is going to be a Jew. I've gotten a lot of bad mail, but it just boils down to what a guy wants to do with his life. People are not going to scare me away from it.

"But the mail started as soon as we were married. There were things like, 'You're gonna be shot at as you walk out of the plane.' There were a couple of threats like that. Then it was mostly black-white. Now there are things like, 'Hitler had the right idea, he ought to do the same thing to blacks that he did to the Jews.'

"Yet I'm not really surprised. Blacks went through the same thing. Only I didn't realize it was the same for others until I read how bad it's been for Jews. But Marilynn's attitude toward it has always been the same as mine. I remember an uncle of hers asking if she was marrying me because I was a star and on top. She said no, she wasn't marrying me because I'm a ballplayer, but for better or worse."

So the Carews have become a close family despite the adversity, and they treasure their moments alone, enjoying each other and their two children. Rod's marriage surely made him a stronger, more mature, and happier person. His old manager, Vern Morgan, is one who noted the change:

"Rod's like a lot of people in any kind of profession. He's grown up since the year I had him at Wilson. He's become a man."

Carew also continued to grow on the ballfield. In 1970 he was off to his best start ever, batting up around the .370 mark when his season came to an abrupt end. The Twins were playing the Milwaukee Brewers. Mike Hegan was on first and took off to second on a grounder. Carew cut over to take the throw from short, then pivoted and fired to first. A second after he released the ball, Hegan barreled into him, leaving the second baseman writhing in pain. Ligaments in his right knee were torn, requiring immediate surgery. He didn't get back until the final few weeks of the year.

The incident upset Rod, who has always been known for his gentlemanly play. He intimated that Hegan could have stopped:

"The play was over; I had already thrown the ball. But he just kept coming."

Carew admitted that the collision caused him to be gun-shy at second for a couple of years, until he was entirely convinced that the knee was back to full strength. He had watched teammate Tony Oliva's career ruined by bad knees, and he didn't want it to happen to him.

The incident also confirmed Rod's way of playing the game. Though he had been hurt, he still never tried to hurt anyone else, a statement many of baseball's so-called tough competitors can't or won't make.

"I avoid hurting someone whenever possible," Carew said. "Reggie Jackson came into second once in 1974 and stood up on a double play ball instead of sliding. It would have been easy to hit him with the ball. But I knew he had a bad leg, a hamstring pull, and probably didn't want to risk sliding. So I went well out of my way to throw around him, and later he thanked me for it."

A player doesn't have to be a brawler to be a winner. In the 51 games he played in 1970, Carew hit .366. Had he not been injured, he undoubtedly would have had an outstanding year and most likely would have taken another batting title. In 1971 he stayed healthy, although he favored the knee somewhat, hitting .307 in 147 games. Then in 1972 he started his string of batting titles with a .318 mark. Finally, in 1973, he had his first super year, batting .350 and getting some of the recognition he deserved.

Part of his recognition came slowly because of the Twins. The team had gone downhill since 1965, and it was now trying to rebuild. Carew was its one shining light, but it's not easy getting publicity playing with a mediocre team in Minnesota.

Yet more people within the game began to recognize Carew's talents, ask him about his hitting, and study his techniques.

"My own theory is to swing the bat," Carew said. "If the ball's around the plate, swing and make contact. It's kind of a Latin tradition. I grew up that way in Panama. Here a lot of guys look for certain pitches in certain areas. But you may never get those pitches. I hate to take a pitch. If I could be a guess hitter I'd hit .500! But I don't like to think too much about hitting. I like being up there, not guessing, just getting up there and swinging free."

Some of Rod's opponents feel that kind of statement is a put on. As ace pitcher Ken Holtzman of the Oakland A's says, "He has an uncanny ability to move the ball around as if the bat were some kind of magic wand."

And Frank Robinson, now playing-manager of the Cleveland Indians, said, "Rod swings the bat about as perfectly as anyone I've seen."

Perhaps one writer summed it up best when he

said, "Although Carew persists in his claim that he is a free swinger who doesn't plot out his hits, the suspicion is growing around the league that if arbitrators demanded doubles that rolled dead exactly 385 feet from the late, or ground balls whose big hops measured exactly 11 feet at the crest, or line drives over the pitcher's left shoulder, Carew would contrive to turn out those, too."

In other words, there are a growing legion of fans who feel that Rod Carew can do just about anything he wants with a bat. Yet Rod still insists he's not all that accurate.

"Hitting is an art, but not an exact science," he says. "Outfielders tend to play me like a right-handed hitter. That leaves me a hole in right field. If I could do it, I'd get a hit every time by just going for that hole. But I can't do it. Usually when I try to pull the ball I hit off my front foot and can't get anything behind on my swing. So I just concentrate on hitting up the middle or going to the opposite field."

Maybe hitting isn't an exact science, but Rod Carew has worked to make his hitting as perfect as possible. The great Ted Williams once said that hitting a baseball was the single most difficult task in all of sports. During the tenure of his lengthy career, Williams hit every chance he had, often begging pitchers and coaches to stay late and throw him more batting practice pitches. Williams said that many of today's players don't do that. They just take the prescribed number of swings in the cage and get out. And as a consequence, their hitting never improves. And using the Williams theory, Rod Carew is a hitter after his own heart.

"I'm different than a lot of young hitters I see today," said Carew, in 1975. "We had a day off Monday, and I took ten extra minutes of batting practice on Tuesday. I take all the extra BP I can get. Guys who are hitting .190 and .220 should be doing that, and they don't. They should be asking questions, and they don't. It's a funny thing about some ballplayers. They get to the big leagues and they stop trying to learn; they don't think they have to try to improve. I've tried to tell some guys the things they're doing wrong. But they just keep doing them over and over again."

There was a time when Carew had trouble with high, inside fastballs. So he worked at it and finally learned how to handle that pitch. He's done the same with any other weakness he felt he had.

"You have to work and discipline yourself," he says. "A guy has to know what kind of hitter he is and has to know his limits. I've seen guys who make an out and come back and break their bats and helmets. Hell, the pitchers are getting paid to get you out, too. I always had the attitude that if a guy gets me today, I'll get him tomorrow."

Another weapon in the Carew arsenal is the bunt. Rod has gotten up to 29 bunt hits a year. He also has used the bunt to get himself out of slumps, much the same way Ty Cobb once did. Understandably, Rod is quite proud of his bunting and the work that goes into keeping that lost art finely tuned.

"Even when they know I'm going to bunt they can't throw me out," he says, forgetting modesty for the first time. "I can drop the ball to a spot where they will have an awkward throw. They have to come up clean with the ball and throw on the run. Not too many third basemen can do that consistently."

In the spring, Rod will practice his bunting upwards of 45 minutes a day, and he'll always take 15 minutes of bunting before every single game. It's the start of his pregame batting practice, which is carefully calculated and shows him to be the true hitting artist he is.

"All some of these guys want to do in batting practice is put the ball in the seats," Rod says. "I concentrate on moving it around."

So he begins, dropping bunts to different spots along the third and first base lines, then between the mound and the lines at varying distances from home plate. After about 15 minutes he starts to swing away—with a purpose.

At first he'll just bounce balls right up the middle of the diamond into centerfield. Then when he's satisfied, he'll adjust his swing and begin cracking solid line drives down both lines, left and right, picking his spots and putting the ball there. Finally, he'll hit some into the outfield gaps and then take one or two roundhouse swings for kicks. As one writer put it:

"For all his modesty about placing the ball, he is as accurate as an archer."

In 1974, Rod made his first run at .400, or at least got a lot of people thinking about it as he flirted with the magic mark right through the end of June. A look at the batting races in both leagues showed something very interesting. Seven of the top ten hitters in the National League and six of ten in the American could be considered Carew-Rose singles-type men. There seemed to be a revival of an old baseball tradition and ancient baseball art—bat manipulation.

Carew himself used a light, 32-ounce bat for maximum handling. This way, he could easily adjust to changing game conditions. There was a late-June game against the Orioles in which Carew was 0 for 4 at bats entering the ninth inning. The horsecollar had dipped his average below .400; besides, he hates so-called "oh-four" games. Since so many of Rod's hits got up the middle, Oriole shortstop Mark Belanger and second sacker Bobby Grich were both cheating, playing close together near the bag. Grich had already taken away a couple of potential hits, one of which would have brought home the tying run a day earlier.

This time Rod wasn't about to get nailed. He waited a split second longer on a pitch and drilled it through the hole at shortstop where Belanger should have been playing. The next night Grich and Belanger moved back to their natural positions, and Carew promptly slammed two hits right up the middle. His average was back to .399 and talk of a .400 season continued.

"If Rod gets lucky and stays healthy, I think he can hit .400," said his manager and former teammate, Frank Quilici. "He has so many offensive gifts. He has great speed and beats out a lot of ground balls. In fact, as far as I'm concerned, there's nobody alive—nobody—who can turn a single into a double and a double into a triple the way Rod can. And when he isn't hitting he can always bunt for hits. Now, after seven years in the league he's really found himself. He's around .400

now, and his hottest months are usually August and September."

Carew didn't really want to talk about .400 at this point. He wasn't ready to put more pressure on himself. "When you set goals you add pressure," he said, "and there's enough of that already. You know, I'm pretty much of a free swinger, and I don't walk too much. I think I walked 62 times in 1973, while Ted Williams had something like 145 walks when he hit .406 in '41. And now, with so many good relief pitchers around, you're always facing somebody fresh. Every team has three or four good starters and a couple of very good relievers. That's a lot of pitching."

The National League's answer to Rod Carew is Ralph Garr, a speedy, freeswinger with the Atlanta Braves. He was hitting about .370 in July of 1974, and was also being mentioned as a possible .400 candidate.

"Nothing is impossible," said Garr, "but for someone like me and Rod to hit .400, we'd have to get about 250 hits. Tough but not impossible. I probably try to hit the ball harder than Carew, so I top the ball a lot, but I beat out a lot of those rollers. I usually just hit the ball where they pitch it to me, but I won't always try to go to left on an inside pitch. And in certain situations I might go for the home run. I take whatever comes."

Carew saw it more as a matter of his job:

"Certain guys on certain clubs have a job to do. My job is to get on base, to try and hit the ball somewhere. On this club we always had guys to drive in runs. But they've got to have somebody on base to do it. Every hitter knows his capabilities. I know mine. I could hit the ball hard if I wanted to. But if I hit 10 home runs I'm not going to help this club. If I get on base and score 95 runs, I am."

Manager Quilici agreed. "Rod could be a different type of hitter if he wanted to. He could hit maybe 20 or 25 home runs. I've seen him hit the long ball. I remember one long blast in the old Kansas City ball park that cleared the equipment house in centerfield, well over 400 feet away. But he never thinks home run. He thinks line drive."

But a .400 season is no easy feat. By late July and August it seemed out of reach, and when the season ended, Carew was "down" to .364, still a better average than most players today ever hope to reach. He also had 218 hits in 599 at bats, 30 doubles, 5 triples, 3 homers, 55 RBIs, and 38 steals. It was certainly a super season, his second in a row, and it was his third successive batting crown.

Carew was a much more secure man than he had been in earlier years. Though not a holler guy, he now considered himself a team leader, who did his thing by example rather than words. It was a far cry from his early days when he took objection to a teammate's remark and the two went into a broom closet to have it out. So many teammates piled in to watch that there just wasn't room for a fight. Finally, everyone just broke up in laughter.

He had the same kind of control and security on the field, as Detroit Tiger catcher Bill Freehan observed.

"Rod has control of his whole game," said the veteran. "He never lets it get away."

With two super seasons behind him, Rod felt he was in line for a big raise. He asked for $140,000, but owner Calvin Griffith offered just $120,000. When neither party would budge, the dispute went to arbitration, where a judge ruled in favor of Griffith. Carew was angered and determined to make up for it with another super season. He was also annoyed by some remarks attributed to Griffith, describing him as an error-prone second baseman and a singles hitter. There was still that old prejudice in favor of the power men.

"I thought I was a member of the Twins' family," Rod said, "but I guess I'm just a number instead. We'll see what happens this year."

Before the 1975 season started, someone decided to compare Carew's .323 lifetime average with that of the late Roberto Clemente after Clemente had played nine years. Clemente, who wound up at .317, did considerably better after thirty years of age. He was just at .303 after nine years. And if that happens with Carew, watch out!

Thus 1975 began, and for the first month and a half or so, Carew was struggling, at least for him. He was hitting *only* .346 and not even leading the league. Then suddenly, Rod Carew got hot, the kind of hot that defies description and boggles the mind.

He began to hit and hit and hit. Hits came in bunches, real bunches, like, say, five straight three-hit games. The whole thing crested in a three-game series against the Yankees when Carew had 12 hits in 13 times at bat. And in one of the games, against newly acquired Yankee ace Catfish Hunter, he blasted two opposite-field home runs, added another single, and drove in all four of his club's runs. And the 12 of 13 was extended to 26 for 42 when taken back a few more games. And that's a .619 clip. Take it back a few additional games and Carew was 35 for his last 59 trips, a .593 average. It was one of the hottest streaks ever and raised his overall season's average to .425. Once again the .400 talk started, but Rod was more interested in talking about his streak:

"The last ten days I've felt so confident that I think there's not a pitcher around who can get me out. I really don't think anyone can hit better than me."

Catfish Hunter, victim of the two homers, wasn't about to argue. Said the man many consider baseball's best pitcher:

"He [Carew] has the quickest wrists I ever saw. There's just no way to pitch him, no way."

Another Yankee hurler, Doc Medich, put it differently. "You just have to hope he makes a mistake," said Medich. "I know that sounds like the shoe being on the other foot, since it's usually the hitter who waits for the pitcher to make a mistake. But Carew's that good."

Writers and reporters again picked up the .400 theme, assembling statements from former .400 hitters. One had remarks made by Ty Cobb back in 1960 which seemed prophetic.

"Somebody will hit .400 again," Cobb had said. "Somebody will get smart and swing naturally."

Bill Terry, another .400 man, had this to say: "To hit .400 you need a great start and you can't

have a slump. The year I did it, I was around
.410, .412 all season, and I was really hitting
the ball on the nose. Hitting is a business. With
two strikes, you really protect that plate."

Then there was Ted Williams, who thought it
would take something else. "To hit .400," said
Ted, "you've got to have power to keep the defense back and spread out. And you've got to be
fast."

Well, Carew seemed to have all the ingredients
mentioned by the three greats except perhaps
power. Yet Oakland centerfielder Bill North, a
man who should know, disagreed.

"There's no way you can play him," said North,
"because he can hit with enough power to keep
you back deep so you can't play him like he's going to drop everything right over the infield. And
he can drop it over the infield. Rod Carew is in a
class by himself."

Others around the league agreed, saying that
Carew had the best bat control of anybody in
baseball.

"He just watches the defense and hits according to how they play him," said outfielder Jim
Northrup of the Orioles.

And Northrup's teammate, second baseman
Bobby Grich, said, "With a man on first and the
first baseman holding, I've seen Rod intentionally
try to pull that ball through the hole."

Oriole hurler Jim Palmer claimed Carew "seems
to hit the ball where he wants to, which is something not too many can do." And Detroit Mickey
Lolich said, "It looks like he tries to take the ball

and dunk it over the infielders' heads or hit it where they ain't."

Carew himself admitted that his favorite kind of hit is "just one inch or two outside a guy's reach. Maybe he cheated over a step in the other direction on me, and I kept him honest."

As for hitting .400, Carew always tried to choose his words carefully.

"It's much too early to say now," he quipped. "But if I'm hitting .385 at the end of August or in early September, then I think I might be able to do it. Last year it got to a point where I thought I might do it, so now I'm trying not to think about it."

That wasn't easy, especially when everyone else connected with the game talked of little else. But, following the pattern of the previous season, Rod gradually dropped off in July and early August, putting a .400 run off for at least another season. Yet he once again produced a year that few will ever match.

Limited to 143 games by some muscle pulls and minor injuries (something that always seems to plague him and could be a factor in a .400 bid), he won still another batting title (his fifth, fourth in a row) with a .359 average, collecting 192 hits in 535 at bats. But the real difference in 1975 was his power. With some of the Twins sluggers from past years gone or disabled, Carew upped his totals to 14 homers and 80 RBIs, the latter figure leading the team. It will be hard for the Twins' brass to call him strictly a singles hitter the next time negotiations roll around.

But it's doubtful if Rod will ever change his

basic style. He likes it too much. He gets as big a
thrill from using his many skills as he does from a
home run. Carew will more than likely remember
the game in which he bunted three straight times
at California third baseman Ken McMullen, who
kept coming in closer and closer and still couldn't
throw him out. The only thing McMullen threw
was his glove; he was utterly frustrated. That will
undoubtedly be a stronger memory than the two
homers, for instance, against Catfish Hunter.
That's just the way Rod is.

As for .400, well, that will probably be the
question every year, especially if he gets an early
hot streak and stays over the mark into June and
July. Some players say he'd do it if he played in
the National League, with its numerous artificial
playing surfaces, which allow for more hits past
the infield. But that, too, might not be a factor,
since Carew seems to compensate for any changing situation.

Rod is still a very quiet, private person. He usually travels by himself to and from the ball park.
In nice weather he makes the thirty-mile trip on a
bicycle rather than by car, and that sounds like
something Ty Cobb would do. He's also very de-
voted to his home life and his family.

"When I leave the ball park," he says, "I'm not
a ballplayer, I'm just Rod Carew—the man—going
out to enjoy life with my family and my friends.
It's only when I get between those two white
lines, when I'm out there playing, that I'm Rod
Carew the ballplayer."

Rod Carew—the ballplayer—is surely the best

hitter of his generation, and perhaps the only one in the major leagues capable of becoming the game's next .400 hitter. If he does, it will surprise no one.